BETTER HOMES AND GARDENS®

COOKING FOR TODAY

BARBECUES

BETTER HOMES AND GARDENS® BOOKS
Des Moines

BETTER HOMES AND GARDENS® BOOKS
An Imprint of Meredith® Books

BARBECUES
Editor: Mary Major Williams
Writer: Janet Sadlack
Associate Art Director: Tom Wegner
Electronic Production Coordinator: Paula Forest
Test Kitchen Product Supervisors: Lynn Blanchard, Jennifer Peterson
Food Stylists: Lynn Blanchard, Diana Nolin, Janet Pittman
Photographers: Mike Dieter, Scott Little
Production Manager: Douglas Johnston

Vice President and Editorial Director: Elizabeth P. Rice
Executive Editor: Kay Sanders
Art Director: Ernest Shelton
Managing Editor: Christopher Cavanaugh
Test Kitchen Director: Sharon Stilwell

President, Book Group: Joseph J. Ward
Vice President Retail Marketing: Jamie L. Martin
Vice President Direct Marketing: Timothy Jarrell

On the cover: Down-Home Ribs (see recipe, page 45)

Meredith Corporation
Chairman of the Executive Committee: E. T. Meredith III
Chairman of the Board, President and Chief Executive Officer: Jack D. Rehm
President and Chief Operating Officer: William T. Kerr

WE CARE!

All of us at Better Homes and Gardens® Books are dedicated to providing you with the information
and ideas you need to create tasty foods. We welcome your comments and suggestions. Write us at:
Better Homes and Gardens® Books, Cookbook Editorial Department, RW-240, 1716 Locust St.,
Des Moines, IA 50309-3023

If you would like to order additional copies of any of our books,
call 1-800-678-2803 or check with your local bookstore.

Our seal assures you that every recipe in *Barbecues* has been
tested in the Better Homes and Gardens® Test Kitchen.
This means that each recipe is practical and reliable, and
meets our high standards of taste appeal. We guarantee
your satisfaction with this book for as long as you own it.

Barbecuing has become an American tradition—on the patio or deck, at the park or beach, and even indoors on down-draft grills. This casual type of cooking is frequently the center of entertaining. For family occasions, it lends itself to more involvement with various family members sharing the job as chief cook. And, this method of cooking helps keep the heat out of the kitchen during warm weather.

Barbecuing can be as simple as you want to make it. Use easy-to-make sauces and marinades to bring out the unique flavors of grilled foods. Or, combine meats with vegetables and/or fruits on attractive kabobs. And, barbecued meats make hearty, tasty additions to salads and sandwiches.

Look over the the tips on the next two pages to get your grilling off to a "no flare-up" start. Then "fire up" the grill and enjoy some of the delicious ideas that follow.

CONTENTS

TYPES OF GRILLS

■ Braziers are designed for direct grilling with a firebox and rack. There are also more elaborate models with hoods, rotisseries, and air vents.
■ Hibachis are miniature-sized grills for direct-heat grilling. They are great for smaller quantities and the size makes them ideal for toting to a park or beach. Most have rack adjustments and air vents.
■ Kettle or Wagon Grills are designed for covered grilling, but also work well for direct grilling.

STARTING THE FIRE

■ For gas grills, follow the manufacturer's instructions. Always be sure to have the grill lid open when lighting. Some grills have spark igniters that will start when the igniter is turned on. Others require a lighted match to be inserted into the lighting hole located at front or side of grill box. The first use of a grill will require longer preheating to temper the coals. Subsequent use normally requires about 5 minutes preheat time to heat the coals.
■ For charcoal grilling, allow about 30 minutes to preheat the briquettes. Self-lighting charcoal takes only 10 to 15 minutes to preheat.
■ Use enough charcoal for a single layer to extend about 1 inch beyond cooking area for direct grilling. For indirect grilling, use enough charcoal for a single layer around the perimeter of the grill. Additional charcoal may be necessary if the weather is humid or windy.
■ To light charcoal, push charcoal into a mound in the center of the grill. For regular briquettes, you can use an electric starter or one of the liquid or solid types of starter. Always follow manufacturer's instructions carefully. Starters work best if you wait about a minute after adding so there is time for it to penetrate the briquettes. Never add more starter after fire is started! And, only use starter designed for barbecuing. Never use gasoline or kerosene! Self-lighting briquettes don't require starter—just light them with a match.
■ When ready to use, coals will appear ash gray in daylight or glowing red at night.

DIRECT OR INDIRECT GRILLING

■ Direct cooking is where the coals are arranged in a single layer directly beneath the food. For highest heat, place coals close together. For more moderate heat, place coals about 1 inch apart.
■ Indirect cooking is where the coals are arranged away from the food so the juices do not drip directly on the coals and cause flare-ups. Arrange the hot coals around the perimeter of the area where cooking will take place. Place a disposable foil drip pan directly under the food. A cover is necessary with this type cooking to hold in the heat and allow the heat to radiate back to the food indirectly.
■ Recipes indicate the timing for each method. Some smaller, quick-cooking foods only have directions for direct cooking while some larger items only include indirect cooking directions. Many items include both directions and you can select the method you prefer.

HOW HOT IS HOT

■ Test the heat of the grill by holding your hand, palm side down, at the same height where the food will cook. See how long before you must pull your hand away and use along with the following as a guide for determining the temperature:
hot: 2 seconds
medium-hot: 3 seconds
medium: 4 seconds
medium-low: 5 seconds
low: 6 seconds

FLARE-UPS

■ Never allow excessive flare-ups to burn your food. Flare-ups are caused by excessive fat and/or too much heat.
■ Reduce flare-ups by lowering the heat. To accomplish this, raise the grill rack, cover the grill, spread the coals so there is more space between, or remove some coals.
■ For excessive flare-ups it may be necessary to remove the food from the grill and mist the flames with a water-spray bottle. Once the flames die down, you can resume grilling.
■ Selecting lean meats and trimming excess fat from meat before grilling will make flare-ups less of a problem. Choose indirect grilling for fatty cuts of meat.

CARE AND CLEANING

■ Clean your grill shortly after cooking. Soak the grill rack and utensils in sudsy water while you enjoy your barbecued foods. If the rack is too large for your sink, wrap it in wet newspapers or cover with wet paper towels. After standing, the rack and utensils should wipe clean. For cooked-on foods, use a stiff brush or a special grill-cleaning brush.
■ Before grilling, remove excess ash to allow for good air circulation around food. Always be sure air-vent holes are not covered with ash. Be sure ash is completely cold before discarding and always place recently used ash in a fire-proof container.
■ Gas grills self-clean the coals if you leave the burner on for 10 to 20 minutes after each use. Occasionally clean the interior of the grill box to eliminate build-up of grease or ash. Follow manufacturer's directions for cleaning.

FOOD SAFETY

■ Always keep foods refrigerated until just before grilling, even when marinating foods.
■ If precooking meats before grilling, transfer immediately to the hot grill. If they must stand before grilling, refrigerate rather than leaving at room temperature.
■ If grilling away from home, pack meats, salads, and sauces with lots of ice in a cooler to keep chilled until ready to grill.
■ Be sure to refrigerate any leftovers promptly after serving.

SWEET ONION BURGERS

A honey and mustard sauce glazes the onion slices as they cook in a foil packet alongside these delicious burgers. For optimal sweetness, select Vidalia or Walla Walla onions.

2   large sweet onions, sliced (12 to
      16 ounces)
2   tablespoons margarine or butter,
      melted
2   teaspoons dry mustard
2   teaspoons honey
1   pound lean ground beef
¼   teaspoon salt
⅛   teaspoon pepper
4   slices Texas toast
4   lettuce leaves
4   tomato slices
      Fresh ground pepper (optional)

For onions, tear a 36x18-inch piece of heavy foil. Fold in half to make a double thickness of foil that measures 18x18 inches. Place onions in the center of the foil. Combine melted margarine, mustard, and honey. Drizzle over onions. Bring up two opposite edges of foil and seal with double fold. Then fold remaining ends to completely enclose onion mixture, leaving space for steam to build. Place packet on an uncovered grill directly over medium coals for 15 minutes.

Meanwhile, in a medium bowl combine ground beef, salt, and pepper; mix well. Shape mixture into four ¾-inch-thick patties. Add patties to grill. Grill patties and onions for 5 minutes. Turn patties. Grill for 8 to 10 minutes more or till no pink remains in meat and onions are tender. To serve, toast both sides of Texas toast on grill. Top *each* slice of Texas toast with a lettuce leaf, a burger, a tomato slice, and *one-fourth* of the onions. Sprinkle with fresh ground pepper, if desired. Makes 4 servings.

To grill by indirect heat: Arrange preheated coals around a drip pan in a covered grill. Test for medium heat above pan. Place patties on grill over drip pan. Place onion packet directly over medium-hot coals. Cover and grill for 20 to 24 minutes or till no pink remains in burgers and onions are very tender, turning patties once halfway through grilling time.

Nutrition facts per serving: 421 calories, 22 g total fat (7 g saturated fat), 70 mg cholesterol, 527 mg sodium, 31 g carbohydrate, 6 g fiber, 27 g protein.
***Daily Value:** 8% vitamin A, 16% vitamin C, 4% calcium, 25% iron.*

DOUBLE SALSA BURGERS

A fresh tomato salsa flavors the beef mixture and also serves as a colorful topping for these zesty burgers.

1 large tomato, seeded and finely chopped
½ cup finely chopped green sweet pepper
¼ cup finely chopped red onion
2 finely chopped, seeded jalapeño peppers
1 clove garlic, minced
1 tablespoon snipped cilantro
¼ teaspoon salt
1½ pounds lean ground beef
2 cups shredded lettuce
⅓ cup finely shredded cheddar cheese
¼ cup dairy sour cream and/or guacamole

For salsa, in a bowl combine tomato, green sweet pepper, onion, jalapeño peppers, garlic, cilantro, and salt. Set aside *2 tablespoons* of the salsa. Cover and chill remaining salsa till serving time.

In another bowl combine ground beef and the 2 tablespoons of salsa; mix well. Shape mixture into six ½-inch-thick oval patties. Grill patties on an uncovered grill directly over medium coals for 13 to 15 minutes or till no pink remains, turning patties once halfway through grilling time. Arrange shredded lettuce on individual plates. Top with burgers, remaining salsa, and cheddar cheese. Serve with sour cream and/or guacamole. Makes 6 servings.

To grill by indirect heat: Arrange preheated coals around a drip pan in a covered grill. Test for medium heat above pan. Place patties on grill over drip pan. Cover and grill for 18 to 20 minutes or till no pink remains, turning patties once halfway through grilling time.

Nutrition facts per serving: 298 calories, 19 g total fat (9 g saturated fat), 87 mg cholesterol, 350 mg sodium, 6 g carbohydrate, 1 g fiber, 24 g protein.
Daily Value: 10% vitamin A, 39% vitamin C, 10% calcium, 16% iron.

BLUE CHEESE BURGERS

Another time, try the easy-to-make blue cheese sauce with grilled steaks.

2 tablespoons plain yogurt
2 tablespoons crumbled blue cheese
1 tablespoon mayonnaise or salad
   dressing
1 teaspoon Dijon-style mustard
1½ pounds lean ground beef
3 green onions, thinly sliced (⅓ cup)
¼ cup chopped green sweet pepper
¼ teaspoon salt
⅛ teaspoon pepper
6 kaiser rolls, split

For sauce, stir together yogurt, blue cheese, mayonnaise or salad dressing, and mustard; cover and chill till serving time.

Crumble ground beef into a large bowl. Add green onions, green pepper, salt, and pepper; mix well. Shape mixture into six ¾-inch-thick patties. Grill patties on an uncovered grill directly over medium coals for 14 to 18 minutes or till no pink remains in meat, turning patties once halfway through grilling time. To serve, toast cut sides of kaiser rolls on the grill. Serve patties in rolls. Top patties with sauce. Makes 6 servings.

To grill by indirect heat: Arrange preheated coals around a drip pan in a covered grill. Test for medium heat above pan. Place patties on grill over drip pan. Cover and grill for 20 to 24 minutes or till no pink remains, turning patties once halfway through grilling time.

Nutrition facts per serving: 414 calories, 19 g total fat (7 g saturated fat), 74 mg cholesterol, 533 mg sodium, 31 g carbohydrate, 0 g fiber, 28 g protein.
Daily Value: 2% vitamin A, 8% vitamin C, 7% calcium, 26% iron.

GRILLED STUFFED MEAT LOAF

The indirect grilling method and a square of heavy foil make easy work of grilling a meat loaf.

1	tablespoon margarine or butter
2	cups sliced fresh mushrooms
1	medium onion, thinly sliced
2	tablespoons snipped parsley
½	cup rolled oats
⅓	cup milk
¾	teaspoon salt
¼	teaspoon pepper
1	beaten egg
1½	pounds lean ground beef
2	tablespoons catsup
1	teaspoon prepared mustard

In a small skillet heat margarine or butter over medium heat till melted. Add mushrooms and onion; cook over medium heat about 5 minutes or till vegetables are tender. Stir in parsley. Cool slightly.

Stir together rolled oats, milk, salt, pepper, and egg. Add ground beef and mix well. Place on waxed paper and flatten to a 12x8-inch rectangle. Spoon mushroom and onion mixture evenly onto meat. Roll up, starting with 8-inch end. Seal seam and ends by pinching together. Stir together catsup and mustard.

Arrange preheated coals around a drip pan in a covered grill. Test for medium-low heat above pan. Tear off a 24x18-inch piece of heavy foil. Fold in half to make a double thickness of foil that measures 18x12 inches. Trim to make a 12-inch square. Cut several slits in the foil square. Place foil on grill over drip pan. Place meat loaf on foil. Cover and grill for 50 to 60 minutes or till no pink remains in meat, brushing with catsup mixture during the last 5 minutes of grilling. Remove meat loaf from grill; cover with foil. Let stand 15 minutes before slicing. Makes 6 servings.

Nutrition facts per serving: 296 calories, 17 g total fat (6 g saturated fat), 107 mg cholesterol, 445 mg sodium, 9 g carbohydrate, 1 g fiber, 25 g protein.
Daily Value: 6% vitamin A, 7% vitamin C, 3% calcium, 19% iron.

BEEF STRIPS WITH PEANUT SAUCE

Marinating round steak in a flavorful marinade scented with pineapple juice and fresh gingerroot makes this economical steak tender enough for grilling.

¼ cup pineapple juice
2   tablespoons cooking oil
1   tablespoon lemon juice
1   teaspoon grated gingerroot
1   teaspoon Dijon-style mustard
2   pounds boneless beef top round steak,
      cut 1 inch thick
¼ cup creamy peanut butter
¼ to ⅓ cup pineapple juice
1   small green onion, chopped
1   to 2 tablespoons chopped, seeded
      jalapeño pepper
½ teaspoon grated gingerroot (optional)
   Green onion strips (optional)

For marinade, combine ¼ cup pineapple juice, cooking oil, lemon juice, 1 teaspoon gingerroot, and mustard; mix well. Trim fat from meat. Place steak in plastic bag set into a shallow dish. Add marinade; seal bag. Turn steak to coat evenly. Chill for 4 to 24 hours, turning steak occasionally. Remove steak from bag, reserving marinade.

Arrange preheated coals around a drip pan in a covered grill. Test for medium heat above pan. Place steak on grill over drip pan. Cover and grill for 28 to 30 minutes or till desired doneness, turning steak once halfway through grilling and brushing occasionally with reserved marinade up till the last 5 minutes of grilling. Remove steak from grill and cover it with foil.

Meanwhile, for peanut sauce, in a small saucepan heat peanut butter over low heat just till melted. Gradually stir in ¼ to ⅓ cup pineapple juice till creamy (peanut butter mixture may thicken at first but will become creamy as more juice is added). Remove from heat. Stir in green onion, jalapeño pepper, and, if desired, ½ teaspoon gingerroot. Cut steak into thin slices; serve with peanut sauce. Garnish with green onion strips, if desired. Makes 8 servings.

Nutrition facts per serving: 234 calories, 11 g total fat (3 g saturated fat), 72 mg cholesterol, 98 mg sodium, 3 g carbohydrate, 1 g fiber, 29 g protein.
Daily Value: 0% vitamin A, 8% vitamin C, 0% calcium, 17% iron.

BEEF FAJITAS

For chicken fajitas, substitute boneless, skinless chicken breast halves for the flank steak.

¼   cup lime juice
2   tablespoons soy sauce
1   tablespoon cooking oil
1   clove garlic, minced
1½   pounds boneless beef flank steak
1   avocado, peeled, pitted, and coarsely
        chopped
¼   cup salsa
1   tablespoon snipped fresh cilantro
1   tablespoon lime juice
¼   teaspoon hot pepper sauce
12   8-inch flour tortillas
2   medium onions, sliced
2   medium green sweet peppers,
        cut into strips
1   tablespoon cooking oil
½   cup dairy sour cream
1   medium tomato, coarsely chopped
        (optional)

For marinade, mix ¼ cup lime juice, soy sauce, 1 tablespoon oil, and garlic. Score meat making shallow cuts at 1-inch intervals diagonally across the steak on both sides in a diamond pattern. Place steak in plastic bag set in shallow dish. Add marinade; seal bag. Turn steak to coat well. Chill 6 to 12 hours, turning steak occasionally. Toss together avocado, salsa, cilantro, 1 tablespoon lime juice, and hot pepper sauce. Cover and chill. Wrap tortillas in foil; set aside.

Tear off a 36x18-inch piece of heavy foil. Fold in half to make a double thickness that measures 18x18 inches. Place onions and peppers in center of foil. Drizzle with 1 tablespoon oil. Bring up two opposite edges of foil and seal. Fold remaining ends to completely enclose vegetables, leaving space for steam to build. Place packet on uncovered grill directly over medium coals for 10 minutes. Remove steak from bag; reserve marinade. Grill steak and vegetable packet on uncovered grill directly over medium coals for 6 minutes. Brush steak with marinade; turn steak. Add wrapped tortillas to grill. Grill 6 to 8 minutes more or till beef is desired doneness and vegetables are crisp-tender. To serve, cut steak into bite-sized strips. Arrange beef, onions, and peppers on tortillas. Top with avocado mixture, sour cream, and, if desired, tomato. Roll tortillas around filling. Serves 6.

To grill by indirect heat: Arrange preheated coals around a drip pan in covered grill. Test for medium heat above pan. Place steak on grill over drip pan. Place vegetable packet directly over coals. Cover and grill for 8 minutes. Brush steak with marinade. Add tortilla packet to grill. Cover and grill for 10 to 12 minutes more or till steak is desired doneness and vegetables are crisp-tender.

Nutrition facts per serving: 539 calories, 25 g total fat (6 g saturated fat), 61 mg cholesterol, 604 mg sodium, 49 g carbohydrate, 5 g fiber, 30 g protein.
Daily Value: 5% vitamin A, 49% vitamin C, 11% calcium, 33% iron.

Rib Eyes with Grilled Garlic

The garlic cloves mellow in flavor as they cook, making a delicious sauce for most any grilled meat or poultry. And for an appetizer, spread the softened cloves over toasted slices of French bread.

1   whole head of garlic
2   tablespoons olive oil or cooking oil
1   tablespoon snipped fresh basil or
        ½ teaspoon dried basil, crushed
1   tablespoon snipped fresh rosemary or
        ½ teaspoon dried rosemary, crushed
2   12-ounce boneless rib eye steaks, cut
        1 inch thick

Tear off a 24x18-inch piece of heavy foil. Fold in half crosswise. Trim to make a 12-inch square. Remove the papery outer layers from garlic head. Cut off and discard about ½ inch from top of garlic head to expose the garlic cloves. Place garlic head in center of foil. Bring the foil up around the garlic on all sides, forming a cup. Drizzle garlic with oil; sprinkle with basil and rosemary. Twist the ends of the foil to completely enclose the garlic in the foil.

Grill steaks and packet of garlic on an uncovered grill directly over medium coals 7 minutes. Turn steaks; grill for 5 to 8 minutes more or till desired doneness. Place steaks on serving platter. Open packet of garlic. Drizzle oil from packet over steak. Lift the softened cloves of garlic from head; spread over steak. Season with salt and pepper, if desired. Cut steak into serving-size pieces. Makes 4 servings.

To grill by indirect heat: Arrange preheated coals around a drip pan in a covered grill. Test for medium heat above pan. Place steaks and garlic packet on grill over drip pan. Cover and grill for 18 to 24 minutes or till desired doneness, turning steaks once.

Nutrition facts per serving: 366 calories, 24 g total fat (8 g saturated fat), 100 mg cholesterol, 226 mg sodium, 2 g carbohydrate, 0 g fiber, 34 g protein.
Daily Value: 0% vitamin A, 3% vitamin C, 2% calcium, 22% iron.

BURGUNDY STEAK WITH MUSHROOMS AND PEPPERS

The mushrooms and green pepper pieces marinate with the steak to enhance the burgundy and herb flavor.

⅓ cup burgundy
2 tablespoons olive oil or cooking oil
2 tablespoons catsup
¾ teaspoon dried marjoram, crushed
¾ teaspoon dried rosemary, crushed
¼ teaspoon salt
1 clove garlic, minced
1 1-pound boneless beef top sirloin steak, cut 1¼ to 1½ inches thick
8 ounces fresh mushrooms
1 green sweet pepper, cut into 1½-inch squares

For marinade, combine burgundy, oil, catsup, marjoram, rosemary, salt, and garlic. Trim fat from meat. Place steak, mushrooms, and pepper in plastic bag set into a shallow dish. Add marinade; seal bag. Turn steak and vegetables to coat evenly. Chill 8 to 24 hours, turning steak and vegetables once or twice. Remove steak and vegetables from bag, reserving marinade.

Thread mushrooms and pepper pieces on short metal skewers. Arrange preheated coals around a drip pan in a covered grill. Test for medium heat above pan. Place steak on grill over drip pan. Cover and grill 10 minutes. Turn steak; add skewers with vegetables to grill next to steak. Cover and grill 12 to 16 minutes more or till meat is medium-rare or medium doneness and vegetables are crisp-tender, brushing with marinade halfway through grilling. Cut steak into thin slices. Serve with mushrooms and peppers. Makes 4 servings.

Nutrition facts per serving: 264 calories, 14 g total fat (5 g saturated fat), 76 mg cholesterol, 182 mg sodium, 6 g carbohydrate, 1 g fiber, 27 g protein.
Daily Value: *2% vitamin A, 27% vitamin C, 1% calcium, 27% iron.*

ORIENTAL FAMILY STEAK

To ensure a tender steak, marinate the meat at least 8 hours, and slice it as thin as you can.

⅓ cup soy sauce
⅓ cup dry sherry
2 green onions, thinly sliced
1 tablespoon brown sugar
½ teaspoon dry mustard
⅛ teaspoon ground ginger
1 clove garlic, minced
1 1½ to 2-pound boneless beef top
   round steak, cut 1 inch thick
   Soy sauce (optional)

For marinade, combine ⅓ cup soy sauce, sherry, green onions, brown sugar, mustard, ginger, and garlic; mix well. Trim fat from steak. Place steak in a plastic bag set into a shallow dish. Add marinade; seal bag. Turn steak to coat well. Chill for 8 to 24 hours, turning steak occasionally. Remove steak from bag, reserving marinade.

Arrange preheated coals around a drip pan in a covered grill. Test for medium heat above pan. Place steak on grill over drip pan. Cover and grill for 28 to 30 minutes or till medium doneness, brushing occasionally with marinade up to the last 5 minutes of grilling. Remove steak from grill and cover it with foil. Cut into thin slices. Serve with additional soy sauce, if desired. Makes 6 to 8 servings.

Nutrition facts per serving: 185 calories, 5 g total fat (2 g saturated fat), 72 mg cholesterol, 512 mg sodium, 3 g carbohydrate, 0 g fiber, 28 g protein.
Daily Value: 0% vitamin A, 1% vitamin C, 0% calcium, 18% iron.

HERB-PEPPER SIRLOIN STEAK

A mixture of catsup, pepper, and herbs coats both sides of this steak, complementing the hearty beef flavor.

2	tablespoons catsup
½	teaspoon coarsely ground pepper
1½	teaspoons snipped fresh rosemary or ½ teaspoon dried rosemary, crushed
1½	teaspoons snipped fresh basil or ½ teaspoon dried basil, crushed
⅛	teaspoon garlic powder
⅛	teaspoon ground cardamom (optional)
1	1½-pound boneless beef sirloin steak, cut 1 inch thick
	Fresh rosemary (optional)

Stir together catsup, pepper, rosemary, basil, garlic powder, and, if desired, cardamom. Coat both sides of steak with catsup mixture. Grill steak on an uncovered grill directly over medium coals for 6 minutes. Turn steak; grill for 8 to 12 minutes more or till desired doneness. Cut into serving-size pieces. Garnish with fresh rosemary, if desired. Makes 6 servings.

To grill by indirect heat: Arrange preheated coals around a drip pan in a covered grill. Test for medium heat above pan. Place steak on grill over drip pan. Cover and grill for 20 to 24 minutes or till desired doneness, turning steak once.

Nutrition facts per serving: 208 calories, 10 g total fat (4 g saturated fat), 76 mg cholesterol, 124 mg sodium, 2 g carbohydrate, 0 g fiber, 26 g protein.
Daily Value: 1% vitamin A, 1% vitamin C, 1% calcium, 19% iron.

GRILLED RUMP ROAST WITH CURRIED MUSTARD

A mixture of mustard, honey, curry powder, and chives makes a glistening glaze for the roast. Then stir the remaining mustard mixture into sour cream for a refreshing sauce.

1 **3-pound boneless beef round rump roast**
2 **tablespoons Dijon-style mustard**
1 **tablespoon honey**
1 **teaspoon curry powder**
1 **teaspoon snipped fresh chives**
½ **cup dairy sour cream**
   Snipped chives (optional)

Trim fat from meat. Stir together mustard, honey, curry powder, and chives. Brush about *1 tablespoon* of the mustard mixture on roast. Insert a meat thermometer near the center of the roast.

For sauce, mix the remaining mustard mixture with sour cream; cover and chill.

Arrange preheated coals around a drip pan in a covered grill. Test for medium-low heat above pan. Place roast on grill over drip pan. Cover and grill for 1½ to 2 hours or till desired doneness (145° for medium-rare, 160° for medium doneness). Remove roast from grill and cover with foil. Let stand 15 minutes before slicing. Serve with sauce and, if desired, snipped chives. Makes 12 servings.

Nutrition facts per serving: 202 calories, 9 g total fat (4 g saturated fat), 81 mg cholesterol, 108 mg sodium, 2 g carbohydrate, 0 g fiber, 26 g protein.
Daily Value: *1% vitamin A, 0% vitamin C, 1% calcium, 18% iron.*

TEX-MEX BARBECUED BEEF RIBS

This two-step cooking process ensures maximum tenderness and ultimate flavor. First, cook the short ribs in simmering water. Then, generously brush them with the zippy, chili-flavored sauce as they grill.

3 to 4 pounds beef chuck short ribs
1 8-ounce can tomato sauce
⅓ cup picante sauce
1 tablespoon brown sugar
1 teaspoon chili powder
½ teaspoon dry mustard

Trim fat from meat; cut ribs into serving-size pieces. Place in large saucepan. Add water to cover ribs. Bring to boiling; reduce heat. Cover and simmer 1½ to 2 hours or till meat is tender. Drain ribs.

Meanwhile, in small saucepan combine tomato sauce, picante sauce, brown sugar, chili powder, and mustard. Bring to boiling; reduce heat. Simmer, uncovered, for 5 minutes, stirring once.

Arrange preheated coals around a drip pan in a covered grill. Test for medium heat above pan. Place ribs on grill over drip pan. Brush with sauce. Cover and grill for 15 to 20 minutes or till nicely browned, brushing occasionally with sauce. Serve with any remaining sauce. Makes 6 servings.

Nutrition facts per serving: 246 calories, 13 g total fat (5 g saturated fat), 74 mg cholesterol, 398 mg sodium, 6 g carbohydrate, 1 g fiber, 26 g protein.
Daily Value: *6% vitamin A, 10% vitamin C, 1% calcium, 19% iron.*

MINTED LAMB BURGERS

Melted mint jelly makes a lovely and easy glaze for these burgers. Warm the jelly over low heat to melt it.

¼ cup apple juice
2 tablespoons dry bread crumbs
2 tablespoons chopped onion
1 clove garlic, minced
1 teaspoon snipped fresh rosemary or
  ¼ teaspoon dried rosemary, crushed
¼ teaspoon salt
1 pound lean ground lamb
2 tablespoons mint jelly, melted
4 pita bread rounds, halved crosswise
4 lettuce leaves
½ cucumber, thinly sliced
1 small tomato, halved and sliced
½ cup plain yogurt

In a medium mixing bowl combine apple juice, bread crumbs, onion, garlic, rosemary, and salt. Add ground lamb and mix well. Shape into four ¾-inch-thick patties.

Grill patties on an uncovered grill directly over medium coals for 8 minutes. Turn patties and brush with mint jelly. Grill for 6 to 10 minutes more or till no pink remains, brushing once or twice with remaining jelly. Open pita bread halves. Line each with a lettuce leaf and a few cucumber slices. Place patties in pita bread halves with lettuce, cucumber, tomato, and yogurt. Serve with remaining pita bread halves. Makes 4 servings.

To grill by indirect heat: Arrange preheated coals around a drip pan in a covered grill. Test for medium heat above pan. Place patties on grill over drip pan. Cover and grill for 20 to 24 minutes or till no pink remains, turning patties and brushing with jelly halfway through grilling time.

Nutrition facts per serving: 375 calories, 16 g total fat (6 g saturated fat), 76 mg cholesterol, 407 mg sodium, 32 g carbohydrate, 1 g fiber, 25 g protein.
Daily Value: 1% vitamin A, 7% vitamin C, 9% calcium, 18% iron.

LAMB CHOPS WITH MINTED FRUIT SAUCE

The robust flavor of lamb tastes even better when accompanied with fruit and mint. We dressed these chops up with a sauce made from orange juice, dried fruit bits, and fresh mint.

2   teaspoons sugar
1   teaspoon cornstarch
⅛   teaspoon salt
1   cup orange juice
2   teaspoons snipped fresh mint or
        ½ teaspoon dried mint, crushed
½   cup mixed dried fruit bits
8   lamb loin chops, cut 1 inch thick
        (about 2½ pounds)
     Fresh mint (optional)

For sauce, in a small saucepan combine sugar, cornstarch, and salt. Stir in orange juice. Cook and stir over medium heat till thickened and bubbly. Stir in mint. Cook and stir for 2 minutes more. Remove from heat. Remove ¼ cup sauce and set aside. Stir fruit into remaining sauce; cover and keep warm.

Grill chops on an uncovered grill directly over medium coals for 12 to 15 minutes for medium-rare or till desired doneness, turning chops once and brushing with the ¼ cup sauce. Serve chops with the fruit sauce. Garnish with fresh mint, if desired. Makes 4 servings.

To grill by indirect heat: Arrange preheated coals around a drip pan in a covered grill. Test for medium heat above the pan. Place chops on grill over drip pan. Cover and grill for 17 to 19 minutes for medium-rare or till desired doneness, brushing with the ¼ cup sauce during last half of grilling.

Nutrition facts per serving: 344 calories, 12 g total fat (4 g saturated fat), 114 mg cholesterol, 180 mg sodium, 21 g carbohydrate, 0 g fiber, 37 g protein.
Daily Value: 4% vitamin A, 37% vitamin C, 2% calcium, 20% iron.

MUSTARD-GLAZED LEG OF LAMB SANDWICHES

Tender, succulent slices of boneless leg of lamb served on a kaiser roll make a delicious entrée for a leisurely backyard picnic. You'll have plenty of time to visit while the roast grills.

¼ cup Dijon-style mustard
2 tablespoons apple juice
1 tablespoon snipped fresh rosemary or
   1 teaspoon dried rosemary, crushed
1 tablespoon soy sauce
1 clove garlic, minced
1 2-pound boneless half leg of lamb or
   boneless shoulder roast, rolled and
   tied
8 kaiser rolls, split and toasted
   Dijon-style mustard (optional)

Stir together ¼ cup mustard, apple juice, rosemary, soy sauce, and garlic. Insert meat thermometer near the center of meat.

Arrange preheated coals around a drip pan in a covered grill. Test for medium-low heat above pan. Place meat on grill over drip pan. Cover and grill for 1½ to 2 hours or till thermometer registers 160° for medium to 170° for well doneness, brushing occasionally with mustard mixture up to the last 5 minutes of grilling. Remove meat from grill and cover with foil. Let stand for 15 minutes before slicing.

Meanwhile, toast cut sides of rolls on grill. Remove strings from lamb; slice thinly. Serve on kaiser rolls. Pass additional mustard, if desired. Makes 8 servings.

Nutrition facts per serving: 304 calories, 8 g total fat (2 g saturated fat), 57 mg cholesterol, 658 mg sodium, 31 g carbohydrate, 0 g fiber, 25 g protein.
Daily Value: 0% vitamin A, 0% vitamin C, 5% calcium, 22% iron.

GRECIAN KABOBS

Take your pick...lamb or pork. Both meats are equally delicious when speared on these herb-scented kabobs.

2 tablespoons olive oil or cooking oil
2 tablespoons lemon juice
1 tablespoon snipped fresh chives or
   1 teaspoon dried chives
1 tablespoon snipped fresh oregano or
   1 teaspoon dried oregano, crushed
1 tablespoon water
1 clove garlic, minced
1 pound lean boneless lamb or pork,
   cut into 1-inch cubes
1 medium red onion, cut into wedges
1 medium green sweet pepper, cut into
   1-inch squares
2 cups fresh mushrooms
   Hot cooked couscous (optional)
   Fresh oregano (optional)

For marinade, combine oil, lemon juice, chives, oregano, water, and garlic. Trim fat from meat; place meat in plastic bag set into a shallow dish. Add marinade; seal bag. Turn meat to coat well. Chill for 4 to 24 hours, turning meat occasionally.

Meanwhile, cook onion wedges in a small amount of boiling water for 3 minutes. Drain and cool slightly.

Remove meat from bag, reserving marinade. On eight short or four long skewers alternately thread lamb or pork cubes with onion, peppers, and mushrooms, leaving about ¼ inch space between each.

Grill kabobs on an uncovered grill directly over medium coals for 12 to 14 minutes or till desired doneness, turning once and brushing with marinade once. Serve over hot cooked couscous and garnish with fresh oregano, if desired. Makes 4 servings.

To grill by indirect heat: Arrange preheated coals around a drip pan. Test for medium heat above pan. Place skewers on grill over drip pan. Cover and grill for 16 to 18 minutes or till desired doneness, brushing with reserved marinade halfway through cooking time.

Nutrition facts per serving: 177 calories, 9 g total fat (3 g saturated fat), 57 mg cholesterol, 46 mg sodium, 5 g carbohydrate, 1 g fiber, 19 g protein.
Daily Value: 1% vitamin A, 29% vitamin C, 1% calcium, 13% iron.

PLUM GOOD PORK CHOPS

Plum preserves make this glistening glaze simple to make. Try it with grilled chicken or lamb, too.

3 **tablespoons plum preserves**
1 **green onion, thinly sliced**
1 **tablespoon soy sauce**
2 **teaspoons lemon juice**
⅛ **teaspoon curry powder**
   Dash ground cinnamon
   Dash ground red pepper
4 **pork loin or rib chops, cut 1¼ inches
      thick (about 2 pounds total)**
1 **clove garlic, split**

For sauce, in a small saucepan heat and stir preserves, green onion, soy sauce, lemon juice, curry powder, cinnamon, and red pepper over medium heat till bubbly. Set aside. Trim fat from chops. Rub both sides of chops with cut side of garlic.

Grill chops on an uncovered grill directly over medium coals for 25 to 35 minutes or till juices run clear, turning once and brushing with sauce during last 10 minutes of cooking time. Makes 4 servings.

To grill by indirect heat: Arrange preheated coals around a drip pan in a covered grill. Test for medium heat above the pan. Place chops on grill over drip pan. Cover and grill for 35 to 45 minutes or till juices run clear, brushing occasionally with sauce during the last 15 minutes of grilling.

Nutrition facts per serving: 224 calories, 11 g total fat (4 g saturated fat), 66 mg cholesterol, 283 mg sodium, 11 g carbohydrate, 0 g fiber, 20 g protein.
Daily Value: 0% vitamin A, 3% vitamin C, 1% calcium, 6% iron.

FRUIT-STUFFED PORK CHOPS
Chunks of sweet apple and snips of tangy apricot fill these marmalade-glazed chops.

1   medium apple, cored and chopped
¼   cup snipped dried apricots
¼   cup raisins
1   tablespoon snipped fresh chives or
        1 teaspoon dried chives
⅛   teaspoon ground cardamom
6   pork loin or rib chops, cut 1¼ inches
        thick (about 3 pounds total)
     Salt and pepper (optional)
2   tablespoons orange marmalade
1   tablespoon dry sherry or orange juice

Combine apple, apricots, raisins, chives, and cardamom. Trim fat from meat. Season with salt and pepper, if desired. Make a pocket in each chop by cutting horizontally into the chop from the fat side almost to the bone. Spoon fruit mixture into each pocket. If necessary, securely fasten the opening with water-soaked wooden toothpicks. Combine marmalade and sherry or orange juice.

Arrange preheated coals around a drip pan in a covered grill. Test for medium heat above pan. Place chops on grill over drip pan. Cover and grill for 35 to 40 minutes or till juices run clear, brushing occasionally with marmalade mixture during the last 10 minutes of grilling. Makes 6 servings.

Nutrition facts per serving: 237 calories, 11 g total fat (4 g saturated fat), 66 mg cholesterol, 54 mg sodium, 15 g carbohydrate, 1 g fiber, 20 g protein.
Daily Value: 4% vitamin A, 2% vitamin C, 1% calcium, 7% iron.

SPICY FRUIT AND PORK KABOBS

Tangy pineapple and cool cantaloupe complement the spicy flavor of this pork on a stick.

2   tablespoons olive oil or cooking oil
2   tablespoons balsamic vinegar
1   teaspoon finely shredded orange peel
2   tablespoons orange juice
¼   teaspoon salt
¼   teaspoon ground cumin
1   clove garlic, minced
1½   pounds boneless lean pork
12   1½-inch cubes fresh pineapple
12   1½-inch cubes fresh cantaloupe

For marinade, combine oil, vinegar, orange peel, orange juice, salt, cumin, and garlic. Trim fat from pork; cut into 1½-inch cubes. Place in plastic bag set into shallow dish. Add marinade; seal bag. Turn pork to coat well. Chill 2 to 4 hours, turning pork once.

Remove meat from bag, reserving marinade. On six long skewers alternately thread pork, pineapple, and cantaloupe, leaving about ¼ inch space between each.

Grill kabobs on an uncovered grill directly over medium coals for 14 to 16 minutes or till juices run clear, turning once and brushing with marinade. Makes 6 servings.

To grill by indirect heat: Arrange preheated coals around a drip pan in a covered grill. Test for medium heat above pan. Place skewers on grill over drip pan. Cover and grill for 18 to 20 minutes or till juices run clear, brushing with marinade halfway through cooking time.

Nutrition facts per serving: 181 calories, 10 g total fat (3 g saturated fat), 51 mg cholesterol, 87 mg sodium, 6 g carbohydrate, 1 g fiber, 16 g protein.
Daily Value: 8% vitamin A, 28% vitamin C, 0% calcium, 6% iron.

DOWN-HOME RIBS

Fresh gingerroot adds an enticing bite to the sauce. Store extra gingerroot in an air-tight container in your freezer and then just grate as needed.

1 medium onion, chopped (½ cup)
1 tablespoon cooking oil
⅓ cup catsup
2 tablespoons orange juice
1 tablespoon brown sugar
1 teaspoon chili powder
½ teaspoon grated gingerroot
4 pounds pork loin back ribs or meaty spareribs

For sauce, in medium skillet cook onion in oil over medium heat about 4 minutes until onion is tender. Stir in catsup, orange juice, brown sugar, chili powder, and gingerroot. Continue cooking over medium heat for about 5 minutes or till thickened slightly. Trim fat from meat. Cut the ribs into serving-size pieces.

Arrange preheated coals around a drip pan in a covered grill. Test for medium heat above pan. Place ribs on grill over drip pan. Cover and grill for 1¼ to 1½ hours or till ribs are tender and no pink remains, brushing with sauce the last 10 minutes of grilling. Makes 6 servings.

Nutrition facts per serving: 313 calories, 22 g total fat (8 g saturated fat), 79 mg cholesterol, 245 mg sodium, 8 g carbohydrate, 1 g fiber, 19 g protein.
Daily Value: 3% vitamin A, 9% vitamin C, 3% calcium, 9% iron.

GERMAN GRILLED RIBS

Apple adds a special flavor to both the ribs and sauerkraut. The sauerkraut heats in a foil packet alongside the ribs.

1	tablespoon margarine or butter
2	medium cooking apples, cored and chopped
1	small onion, chopped (⅓ cup)
½	cup dry white wine or apple juice
2	tablespoons brown sugar
1	teaspoon caraway seed
1	16-ounce package sauerkraut
1½	pounds boneless country-style pork ribs
¼	cup apple butter
	Apple slices (optional)

In a small skillet heat margarine or butter over medium heat till melted. Add chopped apples and onion; cook over medium heat about 5 minutes or till tender. Remove from heat. Stir in wine or apple juice, brown sugar, and caraway seed. Drain sauerkraut; rinse with cold water and drain well. Combine sauerkraut and apple mixture, mixing lightly. Tear off a 36x18-inch piece of heavy foil. Fold in half to make a double thickness that measures 18x18 inches. Place sauerkraut mixture in center of foil. Bring up edges slightly to hold juices. Bring up two opposite edges of foil and seal with double fold. Then fold remaining ends to completely enclose sauerkraut mixture, leaving space for steam to build.

Arrange preheated coals around a drip pan in a covered grill. Test for medium heat above pan. Place ribs and foil packet on grill over drip pan. Cover and grill for 30 minutes. Brush ribs with some of the apple butter. Cover and grill for 30 to 35 minutes more or till ribs are tender and no pink remains, brushing ribs occasionally with apple butter. Partially open sauerkraut packet to make a 5-inch opening for the last 15 minutes of grilling. Serve ribs with sauerkraut mixture. Garnish with apple slices, if desired. Makes 6 servings.

Nutrition facts per serving: 305 calories, 16 g total fat (5 g saturated fat), 65 mg cholesterol, 476 mg sodium, 20 g carbohydrate, 2 g fiber, 17 g protein.
Daily Value: 3% vitamin A, 24% vitamin C, 1% calcium, 8% iron.

SWEET AND TANGY BARBECUED COUNTRY-STYLE RIBS

Serve this summertime classic—pork ribs slathered with a glistening glaze—with other picnic favorites, such as corn-on-the-cob, tomato and lettuce salad, coleslaw, and/or potato salad.

½ cup chili sauce
2 tablespoons apple jelly
1 tablespoon vinegar
1 teaspoon prepared mustard
1 teaspoon Worcestershire sauce
¼ teaspoon chili powder
2 to 2½ pounds country-style pork ribs

In small saucepan heat and stir chili sauce and jelly over medium heat till jelly melts. Stir in vinegar, mustard, Worcestershire sauce, and chili powder; set aside. Trim fat from meat.

Arrange preheated coals around a drip pan in a covered grill. Test for medium heat above pan. Place ribs on grill over drip pan. Cover and grill for 1½ to 2 hours or till ribs are tender and no pink remains, brushing occasionally with the sauce the last 15 minutes of grilling. Serve with any remaining sauce. Makes 4 servings.

Nutrition facts per serving: 449 calories, 28 g total fat (10 g saturated fat), 129 mg cholesterol, 533 mg sodium, 15 g carbohydrate, 0 g fiber, 33 g protein.
Daily Value: 5% vitamin A, 11% vitamin C, 2% calcium, 12% iron.

CRANBERRY-GLAZED PORK RIBS

Ruby red cranberry sauce becomes a tangy glaze in this easy recipe.

1 8-ounce can whole cranberry sauce
   (1 cup)
3 inches stick cinnamon
1 tablespoon Dijon-style mustard
1 teaspoon finely shredded orange peel
1½ pounds boneless country-style pork
   ribs

For sauce, cook and stir cranberry sauce, cinnamon, mustard, and orange peel over medium heat for 5 minutes or till bubbly. Set aside.

Arrange preheated coals around a drip pan in a covered grill. Test for medium heat above pan. Place ribs on grill over drip pan. Brush with sauce. Cover and grill for 45 to 60 minutes or till ribs are tender and no pink remains, brushing ribs occasionally with sauce. Heat any remaining sauce. Remove and discard stick cinnamon. Serve sauce with ribs. Makes 6 servings.

Nutrition facts per serving: 255 calories, 14 g total fat (5 g saturated fat), 65 mg cholesterol, 124 mg sodium, 15 g carbohydrate, 0 g fiber, 16 g protein.
Daily Value: 0% vitamin A, 3% vitamin C, 1% calcium, 5% iron.

FIVE-SPICE PORK TENDERLOIN

To make a green onion brush, use a sharp knife to cut several slits in a green onion from the bulb end.
Then chill it in ice water until the thin pieces curl.

¼ cup teriyaki sauce
1 clove garlic, minced
½ teaspoon five-spice powder
2 12-ounce pork tenderloins
12 ounces fresh pea pods, strings
    removed (3 cups)
½ red sweet pepper, cut into 2-inch
    strips (½ cup)
½ teaspoon finely shredded orange peel
1 tablespoon packed brown sugar
    Green onion brushes (optional)

For marinade, combine teriyaki sauce, garlic, and five-spice powder. Place whole pork tenderloins in plastic bag set into a shallow dish. Add marinade; seal bag. Turn meat to coat well. Chill 2 to 24 hours, turning meat occasionally.

Meanwhile, tear off a 36x18-inch piece of heavy foil. Fold in half to make a double thickness of foil that measures 18x18 inches. Place pea pods and red sweet pepper in center of foil. Sprinkle with orange peel and brown sugar. Bring up two opposite edges of foil and seal with double fold. Then fold remaining ends to completely enclose vegetables, leaving space for steam to build.

Remove pork from bag, reserving marinade. Arrange preheated coals around a drip pan in a covered grill. Test for medium heat above pan. Place pork on grill over drip pan. Cover and grill for 30 to 35 minutes or till juices run clear (150° to 160°), brushing occasionally with marinade up to the last 5 minutes of grilling. Add vegetable packet the last 15 minutes of grilling, turning packet once. Remove pork from grill and cover with foil. Let meat stand for 15 minutes before slicing. Serve with vegetables. Garnish with green onion brushes, if desired. Makes 6 servings.

Nutrition facts per serving: 190 calories, 4 g total fat (1 g saturated fat), 81 mg cholesterol, 522 mg sodium, 9 g carbohydrate, 2 g fiber, 28 g protein.
Daily Value: 5% vitamin A, 63% vitamin C, 3% calcium, 18% iron.

HONEY-GLAZED PORK LOIN WITH CHUNKY APPLESAUCE

Great grilling is a year-round pleasure. Wind up a crisp autumn day by grilling this luscious pork roast.

4 medium cooking apples, cored and
    chopped (4 cups)
¼ cup water
2 cloves garlic, minced
1 teaspoon grated gingerroot
¼ cup honey
2 teaspoons finely shredded orange peel
¼ teaspoon ground cinnamon
1 2-pound boneless pork top loin roast
    (single loin)
2 tablespoons honey
2 teaspoons orange juice

For applesauce, in a medium saucepan combine apples, water, garlic, and gingerroot. Cover and bring to boiling. Reduce heat. Cover and simmer about 10 minutes or till apples are tender. Stir in ¼ cup honey, orange peel, and cinnamon. Simmer, uncovered, for 5 minutes, stirring once or twice. Set aside.

Trim fat from meat. Insert a meat thermometer near the center of roast. For glaze, stir together 2 tablespoons honey and orange juice.

Arrange preheated coals around a drip pan in a covered grill. Test for medium-low heat above pan. Place roast on grill over drip pan. Cover and grill for 1 to 1¼ hours or till thermometer registers 160° to 170°, brushing roast with glaze during the last 15 minutes of cooking. Remove roast from grill and cover with foil. Let stand for 10 minutes before slicing. Meanwhile, reheat applesauce. Serve roast with applesauce. Makes 8 servings.

Nutrition facts per serving: 220 calories, 8 g total fat (3 g saturated fat), 51 mg cholesterol, 41 mg sodium, 22 g carbohydrate, 2 g fiber, 16 g protein.
Daily Value: 0% vitamin A, 3% vitamin C, 0% calcium, 5% iron.

PINEAPPLE-GLAZED PORK TENDERLOIN

This sweet and tangy glazed tenderloin, grilled to perfection, is the perfect dish for just about any occasion from an informal family supper to an elegant dinner party.

½   **of a 6-ounce can (⅓ cup) frozen
         pineapple juice concentrate**
1   **tablespoon Dijon-style mustard**
1   **teaspoon snipped fresh rosemary or
         ¼ teaspoon dried rosemary, crushed**
1   **clove garlic, minced**
2   **12-ounce pork tenderloins
         Fresh rosemary (optional)**

For sauce, in a small saucepan heat juice concentrate, mustard, rosemary, and garlic over medium heat about 5 minutes or till slightly thickened, stirring once.

Arrange preheated coals around a drip pan in a covered grill. Test for medium heat above pan. Place pork on grill over drip pan. Brush with sauce. Cover and grill for 30 to 45 minutes or till juices run clear (160° to 170°), brushing again with sauce during the last 10 minutes of grilling. Remove pork from grill and cover with foil. Let stand for 15 minutes before slicing. Garnish with fresh rosemary, if desired. Makes 6 servings.

Nutrition facts per serving: 154 calories, 4 g total fat (1 g saturated fat), 81 mg cholesterol, 121 mg sodium, 2 g carbohydrate, 0 g fiber, 25 g protein.
Daily Value: 0% vitamin A, 13% vitamin C, 0% calcium, 9% iron.

HAM WITH PEACH SALSA

Perk up your taste buds with this colorful salsa made from sweet, juicy, tree-ripened peaches—the perfect sauce for a thick slice of grilled ham.

1 tablespoon honey
1 teaspoon cornstarch
   Dash ground ginger
½ cup chopped peaches or nectarines
¼ cup finely chopped celery
3 tablespoons orange juice
1 teaspoon lemon juice
1 1-pound fully cooked center-cut ham
   slice, cut 1 inch thick
2 tablespoons honey mustard
   Peach or nectarine wedges (optional)
   Celery leaves (optional)

For salsa, in a small saucepan stir together honey, cornstarch, and ginger. Stir in chopped peaches or nectarines, celery, orange juice, and lemon juice. Cook and stir until thickened and bubbly. Cook and stir 2 minutes more. Pour into a small bowl. Cover and chill till serving time. Spread both sides of ham slice with honey mustard.

Arrange preheated coals around a drip pan in a covered grill. Test for medium heat above the pan. Place ham on grill over pan. Cover and grill for 20 to 24 minutes or till heated through. To serve, cut ham slice into serving-size pieces. Serve with salsa. Garnish with peach or nectarine wedges and celery leaves, if desired. Makes 6 servings.

Nutrition facts per serving: 124 calories, 4 g total fat (1 g saturated fat), 35 mg cholesterol, 908 mg sodium, 6 g carbohydrate, 0 g fiber, 16 g protein.
Daily Value: 0% vitamin A, 34% vitamin C, 1% calcium, 5% iron.

CHICAGO-STYLE HOT DOGS

Serve these jumbo dogs with whole pickled peppers as they often do in Chicago.

⅓ **cup catsup**
¼ **cup chopped pickled peppers**
2 **tablespoons pickle relish**
2 **tablespoons chopped onion**
¼ **teaspoon poppy seed**
4 **fully cooked 4-ounce frankfurters**
4 **frankfurter buns, split**

In a small bowl combine catsup, pickled peppers, relish, onion, and poppy seed. Set aside.

Grill frankfurters on an uncovered grill directly over medium coals for 8 minutes. Turn frankfurters and brush with some of the catsup mixture. Grill for 6 to 8 minutes more or till heated through.

To serve, toast cut sides of buns on grill. Serve frankfurters in the buns and top each with remaining catsup mixture. Makes 4 servings.

To grill by indirect heat: Arrange preheated coals around a drip pan in a covered grill. Test for medium heat above pan. Place frankfurters on grill over pan. Cover and grill for 15 to 20 minutes or till heated through, brushing occasionally with some of the catsup mixture.

Nutrition facts per serving: 528 calories, 35 g total fat (13 g saturated fat), 58 mg cholesterol, 2,052 mg sodium, 35 g carbohydrate, 0 g fiber, 17 g protein.
Daily Value: 52% vitamin A, 68% vitamin C, 6% calcium, 19% iron.

ITALIAN PIZZA SANDWICHES

Some like it hot! If you do, choose the hot sausage. For those with less adventurous palates, choose the mild or sweet sausage. You may want to grill some of each.

1   medium green sweet pepper, cut into
    thin strips
1   medium onion, thinly sliced
1   tablespoon margarine or butter
4   fresh mild or hot Italian sausage links
    (¾ to 1 pound)
½   cup pizza sauce
4   individual French-style rolls, split
2   tablespoons grated Parmesan cheese

Tear off a 36x18-inch piece of heavy foil. Fold in half to make a double thickness of foil that measures 18x18 inches. Place sweet pepper and onion in the center of the foil. Dot with margarine or butter. Bring up two opposite edges of foil and seal with double fold. Then fold remaining ends to completely enclose, leaving space for steam to build. Prick the sausage links in several places with a fork or the tip of a sharp knife.

Arrange preheated coals around a drip pan in a covered grill. Test for medium heat above the pan. Place sausage links and the foil packet on grill over drip pan. Cover and grill for 20 to 25 minutes or till sausage juices run clear and vegetables are tender.

Meanwhile, heat pizza sauce in a small saucepan. Toast cut sides of buns on grill.

To serve, halve sausage links lengthwise, cutting to but not through the other side. Place sausage links in the toasted rolls. Top each with pepper mixture and pizza sauce. Sprinkle with Parmesan cheese. Makes 4 servings.

Nutrition facts per serving: 376 calories, 22 g total fat (7 g saturated fat), 51 mg cholesterol, 1,067 mg sodium, 26 g carbohydrate, 0 g fiber, 18 g protein.
Daily Value: 11% vitamin A, 37% vitamin C, 8% calcium, 14% iron.

MUSTARDY BRATS WITH SAUERKRAUT

A sweet, yet puckery sauerkraut relish tops these spicy brats.

1 tablespoon margarine or butter
½ cup chopped green sweet pepper
1 small onion, chopped (⅓ cup)
2 tablespoons brown sugar
1 teaspoon prepared mustard
½ teaspoon caraway seed
1 cup drained sauerkraut
6 fresh bratwurst (1¼ to 1½ pounds)
6 hoagie buns, split

In a small skillet heat margarine or butter over medium heat till melted. Add green pepper and onion. Cook over medium heat about 5 minutes or till tender. Stir in brown sugar, mustard, and caraway seed. Add sauerkraut; toss to mix. Tear off a 36x18-inch piece of heavy foil. Fold in half to make a double thickness of foil that measures 18x18 inches. Place sauerkraut mixture in center of foil. Bring up two opposite edges of foil and seal with double fold. Then fold remaining ends to completely enclose sauerkraut mixture, leaving space for steam to build. Prick the bratwurst in several places with a fork or the tip of a sharp knife.

Arrange preheated coals around a drip pan in a covered grill. Test for medium heat above the pan. Place bratwurst and the foil packet on grill over pan. Cover and grill for 20 to 25 minutes or till bratwurst juices run clear, turning bratwurst over once. To serve, toast cut sides of buns on grill. Serve bratwurst in the buns and top with sauerkraut mixture. Makes 6 servings.

Nutrition facts per serving: 663 calories, 27 g total fat (10 g saturated fat), 46 mg cholesterol, 1,472 mg sodium, 83 g carbohydrate, 5 g fiber, 22 g protein.
Daily Value: 2% vitamin A, 48% vitamin C, 6% calcium, 29% iron.

RUBY-GLAZED CHICKEN BREASTS

These chicken breasts have such a rich flavor from the currant and apple glaze that you would never guess they are low in fat—only 3 grams per serving.

⅓ cup apple juice
3 tablespoons currant jelly
1 teaspoon cornstarch
¼ teaspoon salt
⅛ teaspoon dried marjoram, crushed
6 chicken breast halves
(about 2¼ pounds total)

For sauce, in a small saucepan combine apple juice, jelly, cornstarch, and salt. Cook and stir till mixture boils. Cook and stir 2 minutes more. Stir in marjoram.

Skin chicken, if desired. Rinse chicken; pat dry with paper towels. Grill chicken, bone side up, on an uncovered grill directly over medium coals for 15 minutes. Turn chicken and brush with sauce; grill for 20 to 30 minutes more or till chicken is tender and no longer pink. Brush with additional sauce before serving. Makes 6 servings.

To grill by indirect heat: Arrange preheated coals around a drip pan in a covered grill. Test for medium heat above pan. Place chicken, bone side down, on grill over drip pan. Cover and grill for 50 to 60 minutes or till chicken is tender and no longer pink, brushing occasionally with sauce during the last 20 minutes of grilling.

Nutrition facts per serving: 167 calories, 3 g total fat (1 g saturated fat), 69 mg cholesterol, 150 mg sodium, 9 g carbohydrate, 0 g fiber, 25 g protein.
Daily Value: 0% vitamin A, 0% vitamin C, 1% calcium, 6% iron.

GRILLED CHICKEN SALAD WITH SALSA DRESSING

A meal in itself—this hefty salad makes for great summer dining. Serve it with tall glasses of iced tea.

⅓ cup salsa
¼ cup mayonnaise or salad dressing
2 tablespoons lime juice
1 tablespoon honey
2 tablespoons salad oil
2 tablespoons lime juice
   Dash ground nutmeg
1 pound skinless, boneless chicken
      breasts
2 8-inch flour tortillas
6 cups torn mixed greens
1 medium tomato, chopped
½ of a yellow or green sweet pepper, cut
      into strips
2 cups peeled, cored, and cubed
      pineapple

For salsa dressing, in a small bowl stir together salsa, mayonnaise or salad dressing, 2 tablespoons lime juice, and honey. Cover and chill till serving time.

For marinade, combine oil, 2 tablespoons lime juice, and nutmeg. Rinse chicken; pat dry with paper towels. Place chicken in plastic bag set into a shallow dish. Add marinade; seal bag. Turn chicken to coat well. Chill about 2 hours, turning chicken once. Remove chicken from bag, reserving marinade.

Grill chicken on an uncovered grill directly over medium coals for 5 minutes. Brush chicken with marinade; turn chicken and brush again with marinade. Grill for 7 to 10 minutes more or till chicken is tender and no longer pink. Place flour tortillas on grill for 3 to 5 minutes or till toasted, turning once. Cool chicken and tortillas slightly. Slice chicken breasts. Break tortillas into pieces. Line 4 individual salad plates with mixed greens. Arrange tomato, sweet pepper, pineapple, and chicken on the greens. Serve with toasted tortillas and salsa dressing. Makes 4 servings.

To grill by indirect heat: Arrange preheated coals around a drip pan in a covered grill. Test for medium heat above pan. Place chicken on grill over drip pan. Cover and grill for 15 to 18 minutes or till chicken is tender and no longer pink, brushing with marinade up to the last 5 minutes of grilling.

Nutrition facts per serving: 426 calories, 23 g total fat (4 g saturated fat), 67 mg cholesterol, 331 mg sodium, 31 g carbohydrate, 3 g fiber, 26 g protein.
Daily Value: 46% vitamin A, 99% vitamin C, 8% calcium, 22% iron.

HERB-STUFFED CHICKEN BREASTS

For direct grilling, cook the chicken with the skin on to keep the meat moist and juicy (you can remove the skin before eating, if you like). For indirect grilling, you can remove the skin before cooking.

1   3-ounce package cream cheese,
       softened
2   tablespoons snipped fresh basil leaves
1   tablespoon snipped fresh chives
1   clove garlic, minced
6   chicken breast halves (about
       2¼ pounds total)
2   tablespoons olive oil or cooking oil
1   tablespoon lemon or lime juice
1   tablespoon water
     Fresh chives (optional)
     Fresh basil (optional)

For the stuffing, in a small bowl stir together cream cheese, basil, chives, and garlic.

Skin chicken, if desired. Rinse chicken; pat dry with paper towels. Cut a slit horizontally in each chicken breast to make a 3-inch-square pocket. Insert a rounded tablespoon of stuffing into each slit. Fasten slit closed with water-soaked wooden toothpicks. Combine oil, lemon or lime juice, and water.

Grill chicken, bone side up, on an uncovered grill directly over medium coals for 15 minutes, brushing occasionally with oil mixture. Turn chicken and grill for 20 to 30 minutes more or till chicken is tender and no longer pink, brushing occasionally with oil mixture. Garnish with fresh chives and basil, if desired. Makes 6 servings.

To grill by indirect heat: Arrange preheated coals around a drip pan in a covered grill. Test for medium heat above the pan. Place chicken, bone side down, on grill over drip pan. Cover and grill for 50 to 60 minutes or till chicken is tender and no longer pink, brushing occasionally with oil mixture.

Nutrition facts per serving: 273 calories, 17 g total fat (6 g saturated fat), 94 mg cholesterol, 108 mg sodium, 1 g carbohydrate, 0 g fiber, 29 g protein.
Daily Value: 8% vitamin A, 2% vitamin C, 2% calcium, 7% iron.

CHICKEN BREASTS WITH BURGUNDY SAUCE

Orange marmalade and burgundy give a wonderfully fruity flavor to these grilled chicken breasts.

¼ **cup orange marmalade**
½ **teaspoon cornstarch**
¼ **teaspoon salt**
¼ **cup burgundy**
4 **skinless, boneless chicken breast
   halves (about 1 pound total)**
   Hot cooked pasta (optional)
   Fresh thyme (optional)
   Orange slices (optional)

For sauce, in a small saucepan combine orange marmalade, cornstarch, and salt. Stir in burgundy. Cook and stir till mixture is thickened and bubbly. Cook 2 minutes more.

Rinse chicken; pat dry with paper towels. Grill chicken on an uncovered grill directly over medium coals for 5 minutes. Turn chicken and brush with sauce; grill for 7 to 10 minutes more or till chicken is tender and no longer pink. Brush with remaining sauce before serving. Serve over hot cooked pasta, if desired. Garnish with fresh thyme and orange slices, if desired. Makes 4 servings.

To grill by indirect heat: Arrange preheated coals around a drip pan in a covered grill. Test for medium heat above pan. Place chicken on grill over drip pan. Cover and grill for 15 to 18 minutes or till chicken is tender and no longer pink, brushing occasionally with sauce during the last 10 minutes of grilling.

Nutrition facts per serving: 184 calories, 3 g total fat (1 g saturated fat), 59 mg cholesterol, 199 mg sodium, 15 g carbohydrate, 1 g fiber, 22 g protein.
Daily Value: 0% vitamin A, 2% vitamin C, 1% calcium, 6% iron.

SOUTHWEST CHICKEN BREASTS

To transform this dish into a salad, slice the chicken breasts and arrange them on plates lined with shredded lettuce. Top with the avocado mixture for a chunky dressing and add some shredded Monterey Jack cheese.

¼ cup dry white wine
2 tablespoons olive oil or cooking oil
2 teaspoons snipped fresh tarragon or
     ¼ teaspoon dried tarragon, crushed
¼ teaspoon salt
6 skinless, boneless chicken breast
     halves (about 1¼ pounds total)
2 avocados, pitted, peeled, and chopped
1 tomato, chopped
1 clove garlic, minced
2 tablespoons finely chopped seeded
     green chili peppers (jalapeño,
     serrano, Anaheim)
2 green onions, finely chopped
1 tablespoon snipped fresh cilantro
1 tablespoon honey
1 tablespoon lemon juice
     Lettuce leaves (optional)

For marinade, combine wine, oil, tarragon, and salt. Rinse chicken; pat dry with paper towels. Place chicken in plastic bag set into a shallow dish. Add marinade; seal bag. Turn chicken to coat well. Chill for 2 to 24 hours, turning bag occasionally.

Meanwhile, combine avocados, tomato, garlic, chili peppers, onions, cilantro, honey, and lemon juice. Toss well to mix. Cover and chill up to 2 hours.

Remove chicken from bag, reserving marinade. Grill chicken on an uncovered grill directly over medium coals for 5 minutes. Turn chicken and brush with marinade; grill for 7 to 10 minutes more or till chicken is tender and no longer pink. Serve with avocado mixture and, if desired, lettuce leaves. Makes 6 servings.

To grill by indirect heat: Arrange preheated coals around a drip pan in a covered grill. Test for medium heat above pan. Place chicken on grill over drip pan. Cover and grill for 15 to 18 minutes or till chicken is tender and no longer pink, brushing with marinade up to the last 5 minutes of grilling.

Nutrition facts per serving: 239 calories, 16 g total fat (1 g saturated fat), 50 mg cholesterol, 130 mg sodium, 5 g carbohydrate, 9 g fiber, 20 g protein.
Daily Value: 3% vitamin A, 24% vitamin C, 1% calcium, 8% iron.

POLYNESIAN CHICKEN KABOBS

Fresh pineapple adds a special flavor to these colorful kabobs. To save time and effort, look for peeled, fresh pineapple in the produce department of your supermarket.

¼ cup soy sauce
2 tablespoons lemon juice
2 cloves garlic, minced
1 teaspoon grated fresh gingerroot or
    ⅛ teaspoon ground ginger
⅛ teaspoon dry mustard
1 pound boneless, skinless chicken
    breasts or thighs
1 medium green sweet pepper
1 medium red sweet pepper
1 cup fresh pineapple chunks or one
    8-ounce can pineapple chunks,
    drained
    Hot cooked rice (optional)
    Green onion brushes (optional)

For marinade, combine soy sauce, lemon juice, garlic, gingerroot, and mustard. Rinse chicken; pat dry with paper towels. Cut chicken into 1-inch pieces; place in plastic bag set into a shallow dish. Add marinade; seal bag. Turn chicken to coat well. Chill for 2 to 24 hours, turning chicken occasionally.

Remove chicken from bag, reserving marinade. Cut green and red peppers into 1-inch pieces. On six 12-inch metal skewers alternately thread chicken, pineapple, green pepper, and red pepper. Grill on uncovered grill directly over medium coals for 5 minutes. Brush with marinade; turn skewers and grill for 7 to 9 minutes more or till chicken is tender and no longer pink. Serve over hot cooked rice and garnish with green onion brushes, if desired. Makes 6 servings.

To grill by indirect heat: Arrange preheated coals around a drip pan in a covered grill. Test for medium heat above pan. Place skewers on grill over drip pan. Cover and grill for 16 to 18 minutes or till chicken is tender and no longer pink, brushing occasionally with marinade up to the last 5 minutes of grilling.

Nutrition facts per serving: 110 calories, 2 g total fat (1 g saturated fat), 40 mg cholesterol, 723 mg sodium, 7 g carbohydrate, 1 g fiber, 15 g protein.
Daily Value: 15% vitamin A, 68% vitamin C, 1% calcium, 6% iron.

CHICKEN AND STRAWBERRY SALAD

Build a backyard brunch around this colorful spring or summer salad. Set out a pitcher of fresh-squeezed orange juice and a basket of blueberry muffins to complete the meal.

2   tablespoons orange juice
1   tablespoon olive oil or salad oil
1   tablespoon lemon juice
2   teaspoons sugar
¼   cup soy sauce
2   green onions, thinly sliced (¼ cup)
2   tablespoons orange juice
1   clove garlic, minced
12   ounces skinless, boneless chicken
        breasts
4   cups spinach leaves
1   11-ounce can mandarin oranges,
        drained
1   cup sliced strawberries

For dressing, in a screw-top jar combine 2 tablespoons orange juice, oil, lemon juice, and sugar. Cover and shake well. Chill dressing till serving time.

For marinade, combine soy sauce, green onions, 2 tablespoons orange juice, and garlic. Rinse chicken; pat dry with paper towels. Place chicken in a plastic bag set into a shallow dish. Add marinade; seal bag. Turn chicken to coat well. Chill for 2 to 24 hours, turning chicken occasionally. Remove chicken from bag, reserving marinade.

Grill chicken on an uncovered grill directly over medium coals for 5 minutes. Brush chicken with marinade; turn chicken and brush with marinade. Grill for 7 to 10 minutes more or till chicken is tender and no longer pink. Cool slightly; slice chicken breasts.

Line 4 individual salad plates with spinach leaves. Arrange oranges, strawberries, and chicken breast slices on spinach-lined plates. Shake dressing; drizzle over salads. Makes 4 servings.

To grill by indirect heat: Arrange preheated coals around a drip pan in a covered grill. Test for medium heat above pan. Place chicken on grill over drip pan. Cover and grill for 18 to 20 minutes or till chicken is tender and no longer pink, brushing with marinade up to the last 5 minutes of grilling.

Nutrition facts per serving: 206 calories, 6 g total fat (1 g saturated fat), 45 mg cholesterol, 1,119 mg sodium, 20 g carbohydrate, 2 g fiber, 19 g protein.
Daily Value: 39% vitamin A, 79% vitamin C, 6% calcium, 18% iron.

ORIENTAL CHICKEN KABOBS

Thread the uncooked chicken on the skewers before you marinate the meat. At grilling time, simply drain the kabobs. Remember to save the soy and sherry marinade to brush over the kabobs as they cook.

¼ cup orange juice
2 tablespoons soy sauce
2 tablespoons dry sherry
1 teaspoon grated gingerroot or
      ¼ teaspoon ground ginger
⅛ teaspoon crushed red pepper
8 skinless, boneless chicken thighs
      (about 1¼ pounds total)
1 teaspoon sesame seed
   Orange wedges (optional)

For marinade, combine orange juice, soy sauce, sherry, gingerroot, and crushed red pepper; mix well. Rinse chicken; pat dry with paper towels. Cut chicken into thin strips. Thread chicken, accordion-style, onto wooden skewers. Place kabobs in a plastic bag set into a shallow dish. Add marinade; seal bag. Turn bag to coat kabobs well. Chill for 2 to 24 hours, turning bag occasionally. Remove kabobs from bag, reserving marinade.

Grill kabobs on an uncovered grill directly over medium coals for 5 minutes. Brush chicken with marinade; sprinkle with *half* of the sesame seed. Turn chicken and brush with marinade. Sprinkle with remaining sesame seed. Grill for 7 to 10 minutes more or till chicken is tender and no longer pink. Serve with orange wedges, if desired. Makes 4 servings.

To grill by indirect heat: Arrange preheated coals around a drip pan in a covered grill. Test for medium heat above pan. Place chicken on grill over drip pan. Cover and grill for 15 to 18 minutes or till chicken is tender and no longer pink, brushing occasionally with marinade up to the last 5 minutes of grilling. Sprinkle with sesame seed after final brushing with marinade.

Nutrition facts per serving: 176 calories, 8 g total fat (2 g saturated fat), 68 mg cholesterol, 584 mg sodium, 3 g carbohydrate, 0 g fiber, 21 g protein.
Daily Value: 2% vitamin A, 12% vitamin C, 1% calcium, 8% iron.

HONEY-GLAZED DRUMSTICKS

Brush the honey-mustard glaze over the drumsticks only during the last 10 minutes of grilling. This allows for a generous coating, but keeps them from burning.

3 tablespoons honey
3 tablespoons Dijon-style mustard
1 teaspoon lemon juice
1 teaspoon finely shredded orange peel
8 chicken drumsticks (about 2 pounds total)
   Lemon wedges (optional)
   Parsley (optional)

For sauce, stir together honey, mustard, lemon juice, and orange peel. Set aside.

Rinse chicken; pat dry with paper towels. Grill chicken on an uncovered grill directly over medium coals for 15 minutes. Turn chicken; grill for 20 to 30 minutes more or till chicken is tender and no longer pink, brushing with sauce during the last 10 minutes of grilling. If desired, garnish with lemon wedges and parsley. Makes 4 servings.

To grill by indirect heat: Arrange preheated coals around a drip pan in a covered grill. Test for medium heat above pan. Place chicken on grill over drip pan. Cover and grill for 50 to 60 minutes or till chicken is tender and no longer pink, brushing occasionally with sauce during the last 10 minutes of grilling.

Nutrition facts per serving: 241 calories, 9 g total fat (2 g saturated fat), 87 mg cholesterol, 370 mg sodium, 14 g carbohydrate, 0 g fiber, 26 g protein.
Daily Value: 1% vitamin A, 2% vitamin C, 1% calcium, 8% iron.

FIREHOUSE BARBECUED CHICKEN

Sweet, spicy, and red describes the sauce on these chicken pieces. Easy to prepare, it's sure to become a favorite with the family and the cook.

½ **cup catsup**
¼ **cup orange marmalade**
1 **tablespoon vinegar**
½ **teaspoon celery seed**
½ **teaspoon chili powder**
¼ **to ½ teaspoon bottled hot pepper sauce**
1 **2½- to 3-pound broiler-fryer chicken, cut up**

For sauce, stir together catsup, marmalade, vinegar, celery seed, chili powder, and hot pepper sauce.

Rinse chicken; pat dry with paper towels. Arrange preheated coals around a drip pan in a covered grill. Test for medium heat above the pan. Place chicken, bone side down, on the grill over the drip pan. Cover and grill for 50 to 60 minutes or till chicken is tender and no longer pink, brushing occasionally with sauce during the last 10 minutes of grilling. Heat any remaining sauce. Serve sauce with chicken. Makes 4 servings.

Nutrition facts per serving: 358 calories, 16 g total fat (4 g saturated fat), 99 mg cholesterol, 504 mg sodium, 24 g carbohydrate, 2 g fiber, 31 g protein.
Daily Value: *9% vitamin A, 11% vitamin C, 2% calcium, 13% iron.*

CRANBERRY-GRILLED CHICKEN QUARTERS

For an easy side dish, cut several small zucchini lengthwise in half. Grill the zucchini halves alongside the chicken during the last 5 to 7 minutes of grilling time.

½ cup jellied cranberry sauce
¼ cup catsup
1 tablespoon brown sugar
1 tablespoon vinegar
1 tablespoon prepared mustard
¼ teaspoon garlic powder
1 2½- to 3-pound broiler-fryer chicken, quartered
   Rice pilaf (optional)
   Parsley (optional)

For sauce, in a small saucepan combine cranberry sauce, catsup, brown sugar, vinegar, mustard, and garlic powder. Bring to boiling; reduce heat and simmer, uncovered, 5 minutes, stirring occasionally.

Meanwhile, rinse chicken; pat dry with paper towels. Break wing, hip, and drumstick joints so pieces lie flat. Grill chicken, skin side down, on an uncovered grill directly over medium coals for 20 minutes. Turn chicken; grill for 20 to 30 minutes more or till chicken is tender and no longer pink, brushing with sauce during the last 10 minutes of grilling. Heat any remaining sauce till bubbly. Serve sauce with chicken. Serve with rice pilaf and garnish with parsley, if desired. Makes 4 servings.

To grill by indirect heat: Arrange preheated coals around a drip pan in a covered grill. Test for medium heat above pan. Place chicken, bone side down, on grill over drip pan. Cover and grill for 50 to 60 minutes or till chicken is tender and no longer pink, brushing occasionally with sauce during the last 10 minutes of grilling.

Nutrition facts per serving: 356 calories, 15 g total fat (4 g saturated fat), 99 mg cholesterol, 354 mg sodium, 22 g carbohydrate, 1 g fiber, 31 g protein.
Daily Value: 7% vitamin A, 6% vitamin C, 2% calcium, 11% iron.

FIVE-SPICE GRILLED CHICKEN

Five-spice powder is a mixture of spices often used in Chinese cooking. Although combinations may vary, the fragrant powder usually includes cinnamon, aniseed, fennel, black or Szechwan pepper, and cloves.

¼ **cup soy sauce**
2 **tablespoons orange juice**
1 **teaspoon five-spice powder**
1 **clove garlic, minced**
1 **2½- to 3-pound broiler-fryer chicken, quartered**
2 **tablespoons honey**
 Hot cooked pasta (optional)
 Carrot strips (optional)
 Cucumber slices, halved (optional)

For marinade, combine soy sauce, orange juice, five-spice powder, and garlic. Rinse chicken; pat dry with paper towels. Place chicken in a plastic bag set into a shallow dish. Add marinade; seal bag. Turn chicken to coat well. Chill for 6 to 24 hours, turning chicken occasionally. Remove chicken from bag. Discard marinade.

Arrange preheated coals around a drip pan in a covered grill. Test for medium heat above pan. Place chicken, bone side down, on grill over drip pan. Cover and grill for 50 to 60 minutes or till chicken is tender and no longer pink, brushing occasionally with honey the last 5 minutes of grilling. Serve chicken over pasta tossed with carrot strips, if desired. Garnish with cucumber slices, if desired. Makes 4 servings.

Nutrition facts per serving: 294 calories, 15 g total fat (4 g saturated fat), 99 mg cholesterol, 607 mg sodium, 6 g carbohydrate, 0 g fiber, 31 g protein.
Daily Value: 5% vitamin A, 3% vitamin C, 2% calcium, 12% iron.

GARLIC-GRILLED WHOLE CHICKEN

A mixture of garlic and basil inserted under the skin and a combination of lemon, sweet pepper, and additional garlic in the cavity flavor every bite of this grilled chicken.

1   2½- to 3-pound whole broiler-fryer
     chicken
3   cloves garlic, peeled
½   lemon, sliced
½   red sweet pepper, sliced
1   tablespoon snipped fresh basil or
     1 teaspoon dried basil, crushed
⅛   teaspoon salt
1   tablespoon olive oil or cooking oil
1   tablespoon lemon juice
     Steamed new potatoes (optional)
     Fresh oregano (optional)

Remove the neck and giblets from chicken. Rinse chicken; pat dry with paper towels. Twist wing tips under the back. Cut *one* of the garlic cloves lengthwise in half. Rub skin of chicken with cut edge of garlic. Place garlic halves, lemon slices, and sweet pepper slices in cavity of chicken. Mince remaining two cloves of garlic. Combine minced garlic, basil, and salt; set aside. Starting at the neck on one side of the breast, slip your fingers between skin and meat, loosening the skin as you work toward the tail end. Once your entire hand is under the skin, free the skin around the thigh and leg area up to, but not around, the tip of the drumstick. Repeat on the other side of the breast. Rub garlic mixture over entire surface under skin. Securely fasten opening with water-soaked wooden toothpicks. Stir together oil and lemon juice; brush over chicken.

Arrange preheated coals around a drip pan in a covered grill. Test for medium heat above pan. Place chicken, breast side up, on grill over drip pan. Cover and grill for 1 to 1¼ hours or till chicken is no longer pink and the drumsticks move easily in their sockets, brushing occasionally with oil-lemon mixture. Remove chicken from grill and cover with foil. If desired, serve on a platter with steamed new potatoes and garnish with fresh oregano. Let stand for 5 minutes before carving. Makes 5 servings.

Nutrition facts per serving: 245 calories, 15 g total fat (4 g saturated fat), 79 mg cholesterol, 127 mg sodium, 2 g carbohydrate, 0 g fiber, 25 g protein.
Daily Value: *9% vitamin A, 28% vitamin C, 1% calcium, 8% iron.*

CORNISH HENS WITH BASIL-WILD RICE STUFFING

A combination of brown rice and wild rice makes for a nutty tasting stuffing. Another time, grill the stuffing packet alongside chicken breasts, pork chops, or salmon steaks.

1   tablespoon olive oil or cooking oil
¼   cup chopped onion
1   clove garlic, minced
2   cups cooked brown rice
1   cup cooked wild rice
¼   cup snipped fresh basil
2   tablespoons grated Parmesan cheese
½   teaspoon salt
    Dash ground nutmeg
2   1¼- to 1½-pound Cornish game hens
2   tablespoons honey
2   teaspoons Dijon-style mustard

For stuffing, in a small skillet heat oil over medium heat. Add onion and garlic; cook till vegetables are tender. Stir in brown rice, wild rice, basil, Parmesan cheese, salt, and nutmeg. Tear a 36x18-inch piece of heavy foil. Fold in half to make double thickness that measures 18x18 inches. Place stuffing in the center of the foil. Bring up two opposite edges of foil and seal with a double fold. Then fold remaining ends to completely enclose the stuffing, leaving space for steam to build. Chill the packet till ready to grill.

Rinse hens; pat dry with paper towels. Twist wing tips under back. Tie legs to tail. Stir together honey and mustard.

Arrange preheated coals around a drip pan in a covered grill. Test for medium heat above pan. Place hens, breast side up, on grill over drip pan. Cover and grill for 1 to 1¼ hours or till tender and no longer pink, brushing occasionally with mustard mixture the last 10 minutes of grilling. Place the foil packet of stuffing beside the hens on grill rack. Grill foil packet directly over medium to medium-high coals the last 15 to 20 minutes of grilling. To serve, cut hens in half lengthwise with poultry shears. Serve with stuffing. Makes 4 servings.

Nutrition facts per serving: 523 calories, 24 g total fat (5 g saturated fat), 102 mg cholesterol, 470 mg sodium, 41 g carbohydrate, 3 g fiber, 36 g protein.
Daily Value: *0% vitamin A, 1% vitamin C, 5% calcium, 5% iron.*

TARRAGON TURKEY SALAD
Some of the tarragon marinade is set aside to flavor the yogurt dressing.

2   tablespoons salad oil
2   tablespoons tarragon-flavored vinegar
1   tablespoon snipped fresh tarragon or
      1 teaspoon dried tarragon, crushed
1   teaspoon sugar
¼   teaspoon salt
1   clove garlic, minced
4   turkey breast tenderloin steaks (about
      1 pound total)
1   8-ounce container plain yogurt
6   cups torn romaine or mixed greens
2   cups sliced fresh mushrooms
2   cups broccoli flowerets
1   small red onion, thinly sliced

For marinade, combine oil, vinegar, tarragon, sugar, salt, and garlic. Rinse turkey; pat dry with paper towels. Place turkey in plastic bag set into a shallow dish. Stir marinade well; add *2 tablespoons* of the marinade to turkey; seal bag. Turn turkey to coat well. Chill for 2 to 24 hours, turning turkey occasionally.

For dressing, stir together reserved marinade and yogurt. Cover and chill till serving time.

Remove turkey from bag, reserving marinade. Grill turkey on an uncovered grill directly over medium coals for 6 minutes. Turn turkey and brush with marinade; grill for 6 to 9 minutes more or till tender and no longer pink. Cool slightly; slice turkey steaks.

In a bowl combine romaine, mushrooms, broccoli, and onion. Toss to mix. Divide romaine mixture among 5 salad plates. Arrange turkey slices on top of romaine mixture. Serve with dressing. Serves 5.

To grill by indirect heat: Arrange preheated coals around a drip pan in a covered grill. Test for medium heat above pan. Place turkey on grill over drip pan. Cover and grill for 15 to 18 minutes or till turkey is tender and no longer pink, brushing with the marinade up to the last 5 minutes of grilling.

Nutrition facts per serving: 208 calories, 9 g total fat (2 g saturated fat), 44 mg cholesterol, 187 mg sodium, 10 g carbohydrate, 3 g fiber, 22 g protein.
Daily Value: 23% vitamin A, 84% vitamin C, 11% calcium, 15% iron.

TURKEY TENDERLOINS WITH HONEY-LEMON SAUCE

In a hurry? These turkey tenderloins can be ready in about 30 minutes. Be sure to light the coals as your first step—they'll need 20 to 30 minutes before they are ready for grilling.

1   large lemon
⅓   cup water
3   tablespoons honey
1   tablespoon catsup
2   teaspoons cornstarch
1   teaspoon instant chicken bouillon
      granules
4   turkey breast tenderloin steaks
      (about 1 pound total)
    Lemon wedges (optional)

Finely shred enough peel from the lemon to make 1 teaspoon. Cut lemon in half. Squeeze *one half* to obtain 2 tablespoons juice; set peel and juice aside. Rinse turkey; pat dry with paper towels. Rub and squeeze cut surface of remaining lemon half over turkey.

For sauce, in a small saucepan combine water, honey, catsup, cornstarch, bouillon, the 1 teaspoon lemon peel, and the 2 tablespoons lemon juice. Cook and stir over medium heat till sauce thickens and bubbles; cook and stir 2 minutes more. Keep warm.

Grill turkey on an uncovered grill directly over medium coals for 5 minutes. Turn turkey; grill for 7 to 10 minutes more or till turkey is tender and no longer pink. Spoon sauce over turkey. Serve with lemon wedges, if desired. Makes 4 servings.

To grill by indirect heat: Arrange preheated coals around a drip pan in a covered grill. Test for medium heat above pan. Place turkey on grill over drip pan. Cover and grill for 15 to 18 minutes or till turkey is tender and no longer pink.

Nutrition facts per serving: 175 calories, 2 g total fat (1 g saturated fat), 50 mg cholesterol, 314 mg sodium, 16 g carbohydrate, 0 g fiber, 22 g protein.
Daily Value: 0% vitamin A, 10% vitamin C, 1% calcium, 7% iron.

APRICOT-STUFFED TURKEY BREAST

Here's a tip from our Test Kitchen: Use kitchen shears to snip the dried apricots. It's easier, faster, and less messy than a knife and cutting board.

1   **2- to 2½-pound turkey breast half with skin and bone**
1½ **cups soft bread crumbs (2 slices)**
½   **cup snipped dried apricots**
¼   **cup chopped toasted pecans**
2   **tablespoons margarine or butter, melted**
2   **tablespoons dry sherry or apple juice**
¼   **teaspoon dried rosemary, crushed**
¼   **teaspoon garlic salt**
1   **tablespoon Dijon-style mustard**
1   **tablespoon olive oil**

Remove bone from turkey breast. Rinse turkey; pat dry with paper towels. Cut a horizontal slit into thickest part of turkey breast to form a 5x4-inch pocket. Set aside.

In a medium mixing bowl combine bread crumbs, apricots, pecans, margarine or butter, sherry or apple juice, rosemary, and garlic salt. Spoon stuffing into pocket. Securely fasten opening with water-soaked wooden toothpicks or tie with heavy string. Stir together mustard and oil; set aside.

Arrange preheated coals around a drip pan in a covered grill. Test for medium heat above pan. Place turkey on grill over drip pan. Cover and grill for 1 to 1¼ hours or till turkey is no longer pink, brushing with mustard mixture during the last 15 minutes. Remove turkey from grill and cover with foil. Let stand for 15 minutes before slicing. Makes 8 servings.

Nutrition facts per serving: 208 calories, 9 g total fat (2 g saturated fat), 46 mg cholesterol, 231 mg sodium, 8 g carbohydrate, 1 g fiber, 21 g protein.
Daily Value: 6% vitamin A, 0% vitamin C, 2% calcium, 9% iron.

TURKEY BREAST WITH RASPBERRY SALSA

Raspberry jam and prepared salsa team up for a sweet sauce with just a little kick.

⅓ cup seedless raspberry jam
1 tablespoon Dijon-style mustard
1 teaspoon finely shredded orange peel
½ cup mild salsa
1 2- to 2½-pound turkey breast half
   Orange peel strips (optional)

Stir together raspberry jam, mustard, and orange peel. Stir *3 tablespoons* of the jam mixture into salsa. Cover and chill jam mixture and salsa mixture.

Remove skin from turkey breast, if desired. Rinse turkey; pat dry with paper towels. Insert a meat thermometer into the center of turkey breast. Arrange preheated coals around a drip pan in a covered grill. Test for medium heat above pan. Place turkey, bone side down, on grill over drip pan. Cover and grill for 1 to 1¼ hours or till turkey is no longer pink (170°), brushing occasionally with reserved jam mixture. Remove turkey from grill and cover with foil. Let stand for 15 minutes before slicing; serve with salsa mixture. Garnish with orange peel strips, if desired. Makes 8 servings.

Nutrition facts per serving: 149 calories, 3 g total fat (1 g saturated fat), 46 mg cholesterol, 147 mg sodium, 11 g carbohydrate, 0 g fiber, 20 g protein.
Daily Value: 1% vitamin A, 8% vitamin C, 1% calcium, 7% iron.

CURRY-GLAZED TURKEY THIGHS

Turn economical turkey thighs into a company-pleasing entrée by glazing them with orange marmalade and dressing them with a yogurt sauce.

⅓ cup orange marmalade
1 tablespoon Dijon-style mustard
½ to 1 teaspoon curry powder
⅛ teaspoon salt
½ cup plain yogurt
2 small turkey thighs (2 pounds total)
   Hot cooked rice (optional)
   Raisins, peanuts, and/or chopped
     apple (optional)

For glaze, stir together marmalade, mustard, curry powder, and salt. For sauce, stir 3 tablespoons of the glaze into the yogurt; chill till serving time.

Remove skin from thighs, if desired. Rinse turkey; pat dry with paper towels. Insert a meat thermometer into the center of one of the turkey thighs, not touching bone. Arrange preheated coals around a drip pan in a covered grill. Test for medium heat above pan. Place turkey thighs on grill over drip pan. Cover and grill for 50 to 60 minutes or till thermometer registers 180° to 185°, brushing once or twice with glaze during the last 10 minutes of grilling. Slice turkey thighs. Serve with sauce and, if desired, rice and raisins, peanuts, and/or apple. Makes 4 servings.

Nutrition facts per serving: 157 calories, 4 g total fat (1 g saturated fat), 30 mg cholesterol, 209 mg sodium, 21 g carbohydrate, 1 g fiber, 9 g protein.
Daily Value: 1% vitamin A, 2% vitamin C, 5% calcium, 4% iron.

GRILLED TURKEY BURGERS

Who says beef has to make the all-American burger? We gave the classic burger a makeover by using ground turkey, glazing it with orange marmalade, and serving it on rye or wheat buns.

1   beaten egg
⅓   cup fine dry bread crumbs
¼   cup finely chopped green sweet
        pepper
2   green onions, finely chopped
2   tablespoons milk
½   teaspoon salt
⅛   teaspoon pepper
1   pound ground raw turkey
2   tablespoons orange marmalade
5   rye or wheat sandwich buns, split
    Shredded lettuce (optional)
    Tomato slices, halved (optional)
    Onion slices (optional)

In large mixing bowl combine egg, bread crumbs, green pepper, onions, milk, salt, and pepper. Add turkey and mix well. Shape mixture into five ¾-inch-thick patties.

Grill patties on an uncovered grill directly over medium coals for 6 minutes. Turn patties and brush with marmalade. Grill for 8 to 12 minutes more or till no pink remains. Toast cut sides of buns on grill. Serve patties in buns and, if desired, with lettuce, tomato, and onion. Makes 5 servings.

To grill by indirect heat: Arrange preheated coals around a drip pan in a covered grill. Test for medium heat above pan. Place patties on grill over drip pan. Cover and grill for 20 to 24 minutes or till no pink remains, turning patties once halfway through grilling time and brushing with marmalade.

Nutrition facts per serving: 289 calories, 11 g total fat (2 g saturated fat), 77 mg cholesterol, 396 mg sodium, 30 g carbohydrate, 1 g fiber, 17 g protein.
Daily Value: 3% vitamin A, 8% vitamin C, 4% calcium, 11% iron.

SPICY SHRIMP ON SKEWERS

For a tangy accompaniment to the peppery shrimp, add fresh pineapple wedges to the grill alongside the shrimp during the last 5 minutes of cooking.

1½ **pounds fresh or frozen large shrimp in shells (thawed, if frozen)**
½ **cup frozen pineapple juice concentrate, thawed**
1 **to 2 tablespoons finely chopped jalapeño peppers**
1 **clove garlic, minced**
1 **teaspoon grated gingerroot or ⅛ teaspoon ground ginger**
¼ **teaspoon crushed red pepper**

Thaw shrimp, if frozen.

For marinade, combine pineapple juice concentrate, jalapeño pepper, garlic, gingerroot, and crushed red pepper. Peel and devein shrimp. Place shrimp in a plastic bag set into a shallow dish. Add marinade; seal bag. Turn shrimp to coat well. Chill for 1 to 2 hours, turning shrimp once.

Remove shrimp from bag, reserving marinade. Thread shrimp on five metal skewers. Grill on an uncovered grill directly over medium coals for 6 to 8 minutes or till shrimp turn opaque, turning skewers once and brushing with marinade. Makes 5 servings.

To grill by indirect heat: Arrange preheated coals around a drip pan in a covered grill. Test for medium heat above pan. Place skewers on grill over drip pan. Cover and grill for 8 to 10 minutes or till shrimp turn opaque, brushing occasionally with marinade.

Nutrition facts per serving: 133 calories, 1 g total fat (0 g saturated fat), 157 mg cholesterol, 181 mg sodium, 13 g carbohydrate, 0 g fiber, 17 g protein.
Daily Value: 7% vitamin A, 31% vitamin C, 3% calcium, 18% iron.

GRILLED SALMON WITH TARRAGON MAYONNAISE

Heavy foil and nonstick spray coating make easy work of grilling delicate salmon fillets. To serve the fillets, simply slide them from the foil to the serving plates.

1   1½-pound boneless fresh or frozen salmon fillets
¼   cup mayonnaise or salad dressing
2   green onions, sliced (¼ cup)
1   tablespoon lemon juice
2   teaspoons snipped fresh tarragon or ¼ teaspoon dried tarragon, crushed
     Nonstick spray coating
1   tablespoon margarine or butter, softened
1   teaspoon snipped fresh tarragon or ¼ teaspoon dried tarragon, crushed
1   lemon, thinly sliced (optional)
     Tarragon sprigs (optional)

Thaw fish, if frozen.

For sauce, in a small bowl combine mayonnaise or salad dressing, green onions, lemon juice, and 2 teaspoons fresh tarragon. Cover and chill.

Tear heavy foil slightly longer than salmon. Cut several slits in foil. Spray foil with nonstick coating. Place salmon, skin side down, on foil. Stir together softened margarine or butter and 1 teaspoon fresh tarragon. Spread butter mixture over salmon. Measure thickness of salmon.

Arrange preheated coals around a drip pan in a covered grill. Test for medium heat above pan. Place foil with salmon on grill over drip pan. Cover and grill for 4 to 6 minutes per ½-inch thickness or just till fish begins to flake easily. Serve with sauce. If desired, garnish with lemon slices and tarragon sprigs. Makes 6 servings.

Nutrition facts per serving: 188 calories, 13 g total fat (2 g saturated fat), 26 mg cholesterol, 143 mg sodium, 1 g carbohydrate, 0 g fiber, 16 g protein.
Daily Value: 6% vitamin A, 3% vitamin C, 1% calcium, 5% iron.

SALMON WITH CUCUMBER-HORSERADISH SAUCE

Leftovers? Combine flaked chilled salmon with leftover sauce for delicious salmon salad or sandwich filling.

4   6-ounce fresh or frozen salmon steaks, cut 1 inch thick (thawed if frozen)
⅓   cup finely chopped cucumber
2   tablespoons mayonnaise or salad dressing
2   tablespoons plain yogurt
1   teaspoon prepared horseradish
1   tablespoon margarine or butter, melted
1   teaspoon snipped fresh dill or ¼ teaspoon dried dillweed
Cucumber slices, halved (optional)
Fresh dill (optional)

Thaw fish, if frozen.

For sauce, in a small bowl combine cucumber, mayonnaise or salad dressing, yogurt, and horseradish. Cover and chill till serving time. Combine margarine or butter and dill; set aside.

Grill salmon on the greased rack of an uncovered grill directly over medium coals for 8 to 12 minutes or just till fish begins to flake easily, turning once and brushing occasionally with margarine mixture. Serve salmon with sauce. If desired, garnish with cucumber slices and fresh dill. Makes 4 servings.

To grill by indirect heat: Arrange preheated coals around a drip pan in a covered grill. Test for medium heat above pan. Place salmon steaks on greased grill over drip pan. Cover and grill for 8 to 12 minutes or just till fish begins to flake easily, turning once and brushing occasionally with dill mixture.

Nutrition facts per serving: 237 calories, 14 g total fat (3 g saturated fat), 35 mg cholesterol, 193 mg sodium, 1 g carbohydrate, 0 g fiber, 25 g protein.
Daily Value: 7% vitamin A, 1% vitamin C, 2% calcium, 8% iron.

SALMON AND SCALLOP KABOBS

Skewer these two favorites from the sea—salmon and scallops—to create a tantalizing meal on a stick.

8 ounces fresh or frozen skinless salmon
    fillets, cut ¾ to 1 inch thick
    (thawed, if frozen)
8 ounces fresh or frozen sea scallops
    (thawed, if frozen)
¼ cup pineapple juice
2 tablespoons lemon juice
1 tablespoon snipped fresh tarragon or
    1 teaspoon dried tarragon, crushed
¼ teaspoon dry mustard
¼ teaspoon salt
2 medium zucchini, sliced ½ inch thick
1 medium red or green sweet pepper,
    cut into 1-inch squares
½ of a fresh pineapple, cut into chunks,
    or one 16-ounce can pineapple
    chunks, drained
    Fresh tarragon (optional)

Thaw salmon and scallops, if frozen. Cut salmon into 1-inch cubes.

For marinade, combine pineapple juice, lemon juice, tarragon, mustard, and salt. Place salmon and scallops in plastic bag set into a shallow dish. Add marinade; seal bag. Turn fish and scallops to coat well. Chill for 1 to 2 hours, turning once. Meanwhile, in a medium saucepan cook zucchini, covered, in a small amount of boiling water for 3 to 4 minutes or till nearly tender. Drain and cool. Cut sweet pepper into 1-inch pieces.

Remove seafood from bag, reserving marinade. On eight metal skewers alternately thread salmon, scallops, zucchini, sweet pepper, and pineapple. Brush with marinade. Grill on an uncovered grill directly over medium coals for 8 to 12 minutes or till scallops turn opaque and salmon flakes easily, turning once. Garnish with fresh tarragon, if desired. Makes 4 servings.

To grill by indirect heat: Arrange preheated coals around a drip pan in a covered grill. Test for medium heat above pan. Place skewers on grill over drip pan. Cover and grill for 8 to 10 minutes or till scallops turn opaque and salmon flakes easily.

Nutrition facts per serving: 150 calories, 3 g total fat (0 g saturated fat), 27 mg cholesterol, 255 mg sodium, 16 g carbohydrate, 2 g fiber, 17 g protein.
Daily Value: 24% vitamin A, 95% vitamin C, 5% calcium, 13% iron.

FISH FILLETS OSCAR

Lemon slices and fresh tarragon scent tender sole fillets and asparagus spears as they cook in handy foil packets. These meals-in-a-packet make for no-fuss grilling and clean-up's a breeze.

4   **3- or 4-ounce fresh or frozen sole or**
    flounder fillets, ¼ to ½ inch thick
2   **tablespoons mayonnaise or salad**
    dressing
2   **tablespoons plain yogurt**
½   **teaspoon snipped fresh tarragon**
1   **pound fresh asparagus**
4   **thin slices lemon**
2   **green onions, thinly sliced**
4   **sprigs fresh tarragon**
    Tarragon sprigs (optional)

Thaw fish, if frozen.

For sauce, combine mayonnaise or salad dressing, yogurt, and ½ teaspoon tarragon. Cover and chill till serving time.

Break off and discard woody bases from asparagus. Cut asparagus into 4-inch pieces.

Tear off four 24x18-inch pieces of foil. Fold each in half crosswise. Trim to make 12-inch squares. Place a fish fillet on each foil square, tucking thin ends under. Top each fillet with a lemon slice. Divide green onions and asparagus evenly among fillets. Top each with a tarragon sprig. Bring up two opposite edges of foil and seal with double fold. Then fold remaining ends to completely enclose, leaving space for steam to build.

Grill packets on an uncovered grill directly over medium coals about 15 minutes or just till fish begins to flake easily. Serve with sauce. Garnish with additional tarragon sprigs, if desired. Makes 4 servings.

To grill by indirect heat: Arrange preheated coals around a drip pan in a covered grill. Test for medium heat above pan. Place packets on grill over drip pan. Cover and grill about 20 minutes or just till fish begins to flake easily.

Nutrition facts per serving: 142 calories, 7 g total fat (1 g saturated fat), 45 mg cholesterol, 108 mg sodium, 4 g carbohydrate, 1 g fiber, 16 g protein.
Daily Value: 8% vitamin A, 34% vitamin C, 3% calcium, 5% iron.

PARSLEY SOLE FILLETS

For a delightful summertime feast, serve these pecan-and-carrot-stuffed fish fillets with a fresh fruit salad. Make the salad from the best seasonal fruit available to you—melons, raspberries, strawberries, peaches, nectarines, or plums.

4　**3- to 4-ounce fresh or frozen sole or flounder fillets, about ¼ inch thick**
2　**tablespoons mayonnaise or salad dressing**
1　**tablespoon Dijon-style mustard**
1　**tablespoon honey**
¼　**cup finely chopped pecans**
¼　**cup snipped fresh parsley**
¼　**cup shredded carrot**
1　**tablespoon snipped fresh parsley**

Thaw fish, if frozen.

Stir together mayonnaise, mustard, and honey. Brush *one* side of *each* fillet with about *1½ teaspoons* of the mustard mixture. Sprinkle fillets with pecans, parsley, and carrot. Roll fish up jelly-roll style. Secure with wooden toothpicks that have been soaked in water. Tear off a 24x18-inch piece of heavy foil. Fold in half crosswise. Trim to make a 12-inch square. Cut several slits in foil. Place fish rolls on foil.

Arrange preheated coals around a drip pan in a covered grill. Test for medium heat above pan. Place foil with fish rolls on grill over drip pan. Cover and grill for 14 to 16 minutes or just till fish begins to flake easily. Brush remaining mustard mixture on rolls; sprinkle with parsley. Makes 4 servings.

Nutrition facts per serving: 189 calories, 11 g total fat (1 g saturated fat), 44 mg cholesterol, 201 mg sodium, 7 g carbohydrate, 1 g fiber, 15 g protein.
Daily Value: 23% vitamin A, 11% vitamin C, 1% calcium, 4% iron.

MUSTARD-GLAZED HALIBUT STEAKS

A simple sauce of melted margarine, lemon juice, Dijon-style mustard, and basil adds a scintillating note to these sizzling fish steaks.

4 **6-ounce fresh or frozen halibut steaks, cut 1 inch thick**
2 **tablespoons margarine or butter**
2 **tablespoons lemon juice**
1 **tablespoon Dijon-style mustard**
2 **teaspoons snipped fresh basil or ½ teaspoon dried basil, crushed**

Thaw fish, if frozen.

In small saucepan heat margarine or butter, lemon juice, mustard, and basil over low heat until melted. Brush both sides of steaks with mustard mixture.

Grill fish steaks on the greased rack of an uncovered grill directly over medium coals for 8 to 12 minutes or just till fish begins to flake easily, turning once and brushing occasionally with mustard mixture. Makes 4 servings.

To grill by indirect heat: Arrange preheated coals around a drip pan in a covered grill. Test for medium heat above pan. Place fish on the greased grill rack over drip pan. Cover and grill for 8 to 12 minutes or just till fish begins to flake easily, turning once and brushing occasionally with mustard mixture.

Nutrition facts per serving: 243 calories, 10 g total fat (2 g saturated fat), 55 mg cholesterol, 254 mg sodium, 1 g carbohydrate, 0 g fiber, 36 g protein.
Daily Value: *14% vitamin A, 5% vitamin C, 6% calcium, 9% iron.*

SWORDFISH WITH CHILI SALSA

To serve grilled sweet pepper strips with the swordfish, place the strips over hot coals the last 5 minutes of grilling. For a colorful plate, choose a combination of green, yellow, and even red sweet peppers.

4 6-ounce fresh or frozen swordfish
     steaks, cut 1 inch thick
1 small tomato, chopped
¼ cup chili sauce
¼ cup salsa
2 tablespoons snipped fresh cilantro
¼ teaspoon ground cumin
1 tablespoon olive oil or cooking oil

Thaw fish, if frozen.

For chili salsa, in a small bowl stir together tomato, chili sauce, salsa, cilantro, and cumin. Cover and chill till serving time.

Brush both sides of fish with oil. Grill fish steaks on the greased rack of an uncovered grill directly over medium coals for 8 to 12 minutes or just till fish begins to flake easily, turning once and brushing occasionally with oil. Serve with chili salsa. Makes 4 servings.

To grill by indirect heat: Arrange preheated coals around a drip pan in a covered grill. Test for medium heat above pan. Place fish on the greased grill rack over drip pan. Cover and grill for 8 to 12 minutes or just till fish begins to flake easily, brushing occasionally with oil.

Nutrition facts per serving: 263 calories, 11 g total fat (2 g saturated fat), 67 mg cholesterol, 412 mg sodium, 6 g carbohydrate, 0 g fiber, 35 g protein.
Daily Value: 11% vitamin A, 20% vitamin C, 1% calcium, 12% iron.

TUNA STEAKS WITH FRESH TOMATO SAUCE

When the temperature soars and the tomatoes are ripe on the vine, fix this fresh-tasting fish dish.

4   6-ounce fresh or frozen tuna, halibut,
       or salmon steaks, cut 1 inch thick
1   medium tomato, chopped
2   tablespoons finely chopped red onion
1   tablespoon snipped fresh basil or
       1 teaspoon dried basil, crushed
1   tablespoon mayonnaise or salad
       dressing
1   clove garlic, minced
¼   teaspoon salt
1   tablespoon olive oil or cooking oil

Thaw fish, if frozen.

For sauce, in a small bowl combine tomato, onion, basil, mayonnaise or salad dressing, garlic, and salt. Cover and chill till serving time.

Brush both sides of fish with oil. Grill fish steaks on the greased rack of an uncovered grill directly over medium coals for 8 to 12 minutes or just till fish begins to flake easily, turning once and brushing occasionally with oil. Serve with sauce. Makes 4 servings.

To grill by indirect heat: Arrange preheated coals around a drip pan in a covered grill. Test for medium heat above pan. Place fish on the greased grill rack over drip pan. Cover and grill for 8 to 12 minutes or just till fish begins to flake easily, turning once and brushing occasionally with oil.

Nutrition facts per serving: 330 calories, 15 g total fat (3 g saturated fat), 73 mg cholesterol, 228 mg sodium, 2 g carbohydrate, 1 g fiber, 44 g protein.
Daily Value: 111% vitamin A, 10% vitamin C, 1% calcium, 13% iron.

MARINATED TUNA STEAKS

Limit the marinating time to no more than two hours. If the fish marinates longer, it will begin to toughen.

4   6-ounce fresh or frozen tuna steaks,
       cut 1 inch thick
⅓   cup dry white wine
1   tablespoon lemon juice
1   tablespoon olive oil or cooking oil
1   clove garlic, minced
2   teaspoons snipped fresh rosemary or
       ½ teaspoon dried rosemary, crushed
1   teaspoon snipped fresh oregano or
       ¼ teaspoon dried oregano, crushed
¼   teaspoon salt
    Lemon slices (optional)
    Fresh rosemary and/or oregano
       (optional)

Thaw fish, if frozen.

For marinade, combine wine, lemon juice, oil, garlic, rosemary, oregano, and salt. Place fish in plastic bag set into a shallow dish. Add marinade; seal bag. Turn fish to coat well. Chill for 1 to 2 hours, turning fish once.

Remove fish from bag. Discard marinade. Grill fish steaks on the greased rack of an uncovered grill directly over medium coals for 8 to 12 minutes or just till fish begins to flake easily, turning once. Garnish with lemon slices and rosemary and/or oregano, if desired. Makes 4 servings.

To grill by indirect heat: Arrange preheated coals around a drip pan in a covered grill. Test for medium heat above pan. Place fish on the greased grill rack over drip pan. Cover and grill for 8 to 12 minutes or just till fish begins to flake easily, turning once.

Nutrition facts per serving: 277 calories, 10 g total fat (2 g saturated fat), 71 mg cholesterol, 106 mg sodium, 0 g carbohydrate, 0 g fiber, 43 g protein.
Daily Value: 109% vitamin A, 0% vitamin C, 1% calcium, 12% iron.

GRILLED POTATO SKINS

Serve these crispy taters as an appetizer or a side dish. To save time, follow the instructions for micro-cooking the potatoes in the first step (see note).

6   baking potatoes (about 8 ounces each)
2   tablespoons margarine or butter, melted
½   cup picante sauce
1   cup shredded cheddar cheese, (4 ounces)
3   slices bacon, crisp-cooked and crumbled, or ½ cup finely chopped fully cooked ham
    Chopped tomato (optional)
    Sliced green onion (optional)
½   cup dairy sour cream

Scrub potatoes; prick with a fork. Tear off six 18x9-inch pieces of heavy foil. Fold each in half to make a 9x9-inch square. Wrap each potato in a foil square. Grill on an uncovered grill directly over medium-slow coals for 1 to 2 hours or till tender.* Unwrap potatoes. Cool enough to handle.

Cut potatoes in half lengthwise. Scoop out potato pulp, leaving ¼-inch-thick shell. (Save potato pulp for another use.) Brush the inside of each potato shell with melted margarine. Spoon 2 teaspoons picante sauce into each potato shell. Sprinkle each with cheese. Add bacon or ham.

Grill potato skins on an uncovered grill directly over medium coals for 10 to 12 minutes or till skins are crisp. Sprinkle with tomato and green onion, if desired. Top with sour cream. Makes 12 servings.

Note: Potatoes may be baked or micro-cooked to this point. *To bake:* Prick potatoes with a fork. Bake in a 375° oven for 50 to 60 minutes or till tender. *To micro-cook:* Place *3* of the pricked potatoes in the microwave oven. Micro-cook on 100% power (high) for 13 to 16 minutes or till tender, rearranging once after 7 minutes. Repeat with remaining potatoes.

Nutrition facts per serving: 166 calories, 8 g total fat (4 g saturated fat), 16 mg cholesterol, 190 mg sodium, 19 g carbohydrate, 1 g fiber, 5 g protein. Daily Value: 8% vitamin A, 24% vitamin C, 7% calcium, 7% iron.

ROSEMARY NEW POTATOES

Purchase a disposable foil pan to grill the potatoes. Or, make a pan using a 12-inch square of double thickness of heavy foil. Fold up the sides to make a pan.

1 pound small new potatoes, halved
2 tablespoons margarine or butter, melted
2 teaspoons snipped fresh rosemary or ½ teaspoon dried rosemary, crushed
⅛ teaspoon chili powder
1 tablespoon snipped fresh chives

In a greased 8x8x2-inch foil pan, arrange raw potatoes. Stir together margarine or butter, rosemary, and chili powder. Pour over potatoes; toss to coat.

Arrange preheated coals around a drip pan in a covered grill. Test for medium-hot heat above the pan. Place foil pan containing potatoes over the drip pan. Cover and grill for 25 minutes. Add chives; cover and grill for 5 to 10 minutes more or till potatoes are tender. Season with salt and pepper, if desired. Makes 4 servings.

Nutrition facts per serving: 171 calories, 7 g total fat (1 g saturated fat), 0 mg cholesterol, 143 mg sodium, 25 g carbohydrate, 1 g fiber, 3 g protein.
Daily Value: 7% vitamin A, 25% vitamin C, 1% calcium, 12% iron.

PILAF IN PEPPERS

Sweet pepper halves make colorful holders for a brown rice and vegetable combo. Grill them with pork chops, meaty chicken pieces, or turkey tenderloin steaks over indirect heat.

2   cups water
1   cup regular brown rice
½   cup chopped celery
½   cup shredded carrot
4   green onions, sliced
1   tablespoon margarine or butter
2   teaspoons instant chicken bouillon
      granules
⅛   teaspoon pepper
3   medium green, red, and/or yellow
      sweet peppers

In a medium saucepan combine water, brown rice, celery, carrot, green onions, margarine or butter, bouillon granules, and pepper. Bring to boiling; reduce heat. Cover and simmer about 35 minutes or till rice is tender.

Meanwhile, cut sweet peppers in half lengthwise. Cut away stem and membrane. Place pepper halves, cut side up in two foil pie pans or one 13x9-inch foil pan. Spoon rice mixture into peppers, mounding as necessary. Cover pan(s) with foil.

Arrange preheated coals around a drip pan in a covered grill. Test for medium heat above pan. Place foil pan(s) containing pepper halves over drip pan. Cover and grill for 20 to 25 minutes or till peppers are tender and rice is heated through. Makes 6 serving.

Nutrition facts per serving: 150 calories, 3 g total fat (1 g saturated fat), 0 mg cholesterol, 328 mg sodium, 28 g carbohydrate, 3 g fiber, 3 g protein.
Daily Value: *32% vitamin A, 50% vitamin C, 1% calcium, 5% iron.*

HERB-GRILLED TOMATOES

For a sumptuous match, pair these Parmesan-crowned tomatoes with a thick, juicy steak.

4   small tomatoes
3   tablespoons dairy sour cream or plain
    yogurt
1   tablespoon snipped fresh basil or
    1 teaspoon dried basil, crushed
1   tablespoon fine dry bread crumbs
1   tablespoon finely shredded or grated
    Parmesan cheese
    Fresh basil (optional)

Remove cores from tomatoes and cut tomatoes in half crosswise. Spread cut side of each tomato with sour cream or yogurt. Sprinkle each with basil. Sprinkle bread crumbs and Parmesan cheese on tomatoes. Arrange tomato halves in a foil pie pan.

Arrange preheated coals around a drip pan in a covered grill. Test for medium heat above the pan. Place the foil pan containing tomatoes on grill over drip pan. Cover and grill for 10 to 15 minutes or till tomatoes are heated through. Garnish with fresh basil, if desired. Makes 4 servings.

Herb-Grilled Roma Tomatoes: Prepare as directed above except substitute 4 roma tomatoes for the tomatoes. *Do not* core tomatoes. Cut lengthwise in half.

Nutrition facts per serving: 56 calories, 3 g total fat (1 g saturated fat), 6 mg cholesterol, 46 mg sodium, 6 g carbohydrate, 1 g fiber, 2 g protein.
Daily Value: *8% vitamin A, 29% vitamin C, 2% calcium, 3% iron.*

STUFFED EGGPLANT

Perfect with either chicken or pork, these eggplant shells brimming with mushrooms, sweet pepper, and tomato combine the best of summer's bounty.

1   medium eggplant
1   cup sliced fresh mushrooms
½   cup chopped green sweet pepper
1   small onion, finely chopped
1   clove garlic, minced
½   teaspoon dried basil, crushed
1   tablespoon olive oil or cooking oil
1   medium tomato, chopped
½   teaspoon salt
¼   cup finely shredded or grated
       Parmesan cheese

Cut eggplant in half lengthwise. Using a grapefruit knife, hollow out eggplant, leaving a ¼-inch-thick shell. Chop eggplant pulp (you should have about 2½ cups).

In a large skillet cook mushrooms, green pepper, onion, garlic, basil, and chopped eggplant in oil over medium heat till nearly tender, stirring occasionally. Stir in tomato and salt. Spoon mixture into eggplant shells. Sprinkle with Parmesan cheese.

Tear two 18x24-inch pieces of heavy foil. Fold each piece in half to make two double thicknesses of foil that measure 18x12 inches. Place an eggplant half on each. Bring up two opposite edges of each foil and seal with a double fold. Then fold remaining ends to completely enclose eggplant halves, leaving space for steam to build.

Arrange preheated coals around a drip pan in a covered grill. Test for medium heat above pan. Place eggplant packets on grill over drip pan. Cover and grill about 20 minutes or till eggplant shells are tender. Makes 4 servings.

Nutrition facts per serving: 107 calories, 6 g total fat (1 g saturated fat), 5 mg cholesterol, 353 mg sodium, 12 g carbohydrate, 4 g fiber, 5 g protein.
Daily Value: *4% vitamin A, 30% vitamin C, 6% calcium, 6% iron.*

ONION BLOSSOMS

Dress up any barbecued meat, poultry, or fish with these sweet onions cut to resemble flowers. Choose Vidalia, Walla Walla, or other locally available sweet onions.

4   medium sweet onions (4 to 5 ounces each)
1   tablespoon margarine or butter, melted
1   teaspoon Dijon-style mustard
⅛   teaspoon hot pepper sauce
1   tablespoon brown sugar
     Pepper

Peel onions; cut almost through each onion forming 8 wedges. Tear off four 24x18-inch pieces of heavy foil. Fold each in half crosswise. Trim to make 12-inch squares. Place an onion in the center of each foil square. Stir together margarine or butter, mustard, and hot pepper sauce. Drizzle mixture over onions. Sprinkle with brown sugar. Bring up two opposite edges of each foil square and seal with double fold. Then fold remaining ends to completely enclose each onion, leaving space for steam to build.

Arrange preheated coals around drip pan in a covered grill. Test for medium heat above pan. Place foil packets on grill over drip pan. Cover and grill for 25 minutes or till onions are nearly tender. Make a 2-inch opening in the top of each packet. Cover and grill for 10 minutes more or till onions are lightly browned. Sprinkle with pepper. Makes 4 servings.

Nutrition facts per serving: 83 calories, 3 g total fat (1 g saturated fat), 0 mg cholesterol, 70 mg sodium, 13 g carbohydrate, 2 g fiber, 1 g protein.
Daily Value: *3% vitamin A, 8% vitamin C, 2% calcium, 2% iron.*

SOUTH SEAS PINEAPPLE

These curried pineapple slices add a tropical touch to your backyard barbecue.

1   medium pineapple
1   tablespoon margarine or butter,
        melted
1   tablespoon packed brown sugar
¼   teaspoon curry powder
½   cup plain yogurt
2   tablespoons toasted coconut

Cut pineapple crosswise into six ¾-inch-thick slices. Stir together margarine or butter, brown sugar, and curry powder.

Grill pineapple slices on an uncovered grill directly over medium coals for 6 to 8 minutes or till heated through, turning once and brushing once or twice with margarine mixture. To serve, cut slices in half. Serve warm topped with yogurt and coconut. Makes 6 servings.

Nutrition facts per serving: 53 calories, 3 g total fat (1 g saturated fat), 2 mg cholesterol, 40 mg sodium, 5 g carbohydrate, 0 g fiber, 1 g protein.
Daily Value: 2% vitamin A, 1% vitamin C, 3% calcium, 0% iron.

GRILLED FRENCH BREAD

You have absolutely no need to turn on your oven with this easy way to serve warm, crusty French bread.

¼ cup margarine or butter
2 tablespoons snipped fresh parsley
1 clove garlic, minced
⅛ teaspoon ground red pepper
    (optional)
¼ cup grated Parmesan cheese
1 16-ounce loaf unsliced French bread

In a medium skillet combine margarine or butter, parsley, garlic, and, if desired, red pepper. Heat over medium heat until margarine is melted. Stir in Parmesan cheese. Cut French bread in half lengthwise.

Place bread, cut side down, on an uncovered grill directly over medium coals. Grill about 2 minutes or till toasted. Turn cut side up. Brush with margarine mixture. Grill for 1 to 2 minutes more. To serve, cut into 2-inch slices. Makes 8 to 10 servings.

Nutrition facts per serving: 223 calories, 8 g total fat (2 g saturated fat), 2 mg cholesterol, 471 mg sodium, 30 g carbohydrate, 0 g fiber, 6 g protein.
Daily Value: 8% vitamin A, 2% vitamin C, 7% calcium, 10% iron.

Keep track of your daily nutrition needs by using the information we provide at the end of each recipe. We've analyzed the nutritional content of each recipe serving for you. When a recipe gives an ingredient substitution, we used the first choice in the analysis. If it makes a range of servings (such as 4 to 6), we used the smallest number. Ingredients listed as optional weren't included in the calculations.

METRIC COOKING HINTS

By making a few conversions, cooks in Australia, Canada, and the United Kingdom can use the recipes in Better Homes and Gardens® *Barbecues* with confidence. The charts on this page provide a guide for converting measurements from the U.S. customary system, which is used throughout this book, to the imperial and metric systems. There also is a conversion table for oven temperatures to accommodate the differences in oven calibrations.

Volume and Weight: Americans traditionally use cup measures for liquid and solid ingredients. The chart (top right) shows the approximate imperial and metric equivalents. If you are accustomed to weighing solid ingredients, here are some helpful approximate equivalents.
- 1 cup butter, caster sugar, or rice = 8 ounces = about 250 grams
- 1 cup flour = 4 ounces = about 125 grams
- 1 cup icing sugar = 5 ounces = about 150 grams
  Spoon measures are used for smaller amounts of ingredients. Although the size of the tablespoon varies slightly among countries, for practical purposes and for recipes in this book, a straight substitution is all that's necessary.
  Measurements made using cups or spoons should always be level, unless stated otherwise.

Product Differences: Most of the ingredients called for in the recipes in this book are available in English-speaking countries. However, some are known by different names. Here are some common American ingredients and their possible counterparts:
- Sugar is granulated or caster sugar.
- Powdered sugar is icing sugar.
- All-purpose flour is plain household flour or white flour. When self-rising flour is used in place of all-purpose flour in a recipe that calls for leavening, omit the leavening agent (baking soda or baking powder) and salt.
- Light corn syrup is golden syrup.
- Cornstarch is cornflour.
- Baking soda is bicarbonate of soda.
- Vanilla is vanilla essence.

USEFUL EQUIVALENTS

⅛ teaspoon = 0.5 ml
¼ teaspoon = 1 ml
½ teaspoon = 2 ml
1 teaspoon = 5 ml
¼ cup = 2 fluid ounces = 50 ml
⅓ cup = 3 fluid ounces = 75 ml
½ cup = 4 fluid ounces = 125 ml
⅔ cup = 5 fluid ounces = 150 ml
¾ cup = 6 fluid ounces = 175 ml
1 cup = 8 fluid ounces = 250 ml
2 cups = 1 pint
2 pints = 1 litre
½ inch = 1 centimetre
1 inch = 2 centimetres

BAKING PAN SIZES

American	Metric
8x1½-inch round baking pan	20x4-centimetre sandwich or cake tin
9x1½-inch round baking pan	23x3.5-centimetre sandwich or cake tin
11x7x1½-inch baking pan	28x18x4-centimetre baking pan
13x9x2-inch baking pan	32.5x23x5-centimetre baking pan
2-quart rectangular baking dish	30x19x5-centimetre baking pan
15x10x2-inch baking pan	38x25.5x2.5-centimetre baking pan (Swiss roll tin)
9-inch pie plate	22x4- or 23x4-centimetre pie plate
7- or 8-inch springform pan	18- or 20-centimetre springform or loose-bottom cake tin
9x5x3-inch loaf pan	23x13x6-centimetre or 2-pound narrow loaf pan or paté tin
1½-quart casserole	1.5-litre casserole
2-quart casserole	2-litre casserole

OVEN TEMPERATURE EQUIVALENTS

Fahrenheit Setting	Celsius Setting*	Gas Setting
300°F	150°C	Gas Mark 2
325°F	160°C	Gas Mark 3
350°F	180°C	Gas Mark 4
375°F	190°C	Gas Mark 5
400°F	200°C	Gas Mark 6
425°F	220°C	Gas Mark 7
450°F	230°C	Gas Mark 8
Broil		Grill

Electric and gas ovens may be calibrated using Celsius. However, increase the Celsius setting 10 to 20 degrees when cooking above 160°C with an electric oven. For convection or forced-air ovens (gas or electric), lower the temperature setting 10°C when cooking at all heat levels.